DAVID
WILLIAMSON'S
JACK
MANNING
TRILOGY

A
STUDY
GUIDE

DAVID MOORE

CURRENCY PRESS, SYDNEY

First published in 2003 by
Currency Press
PO Box 2287
Strawberry Hills NSW 2012 Australia
enquiries@currency.com.au
www.currency.com.au

Copying for Educational Purposes:
The Australian *Copyright Act* 1968 allows a maximum of one chapter or
10% of this book, whichever is the greater, to be copied by any
educational institution for its educational purposes provided that the
educational institution (or the body that administers it) has given a
remuneration notice to Copyright Agency Limited (CAL) under the
Act. For details of the CAL licence for educational institutions please
contact CAL, 19/157 Liverpool Street, Sydney, NSW 2000, tel (02) 9394
7600, fax (02) 9394 7601, email: info@copyright.com.au.

Copying for Other Purposes:
Except as permitted under the Act, for example a fair dealing for the
purposes of study, research, criticism or review, no part of this book may
be reproduced, stored in a retrieval system, or transmitted in any form
or by any means without prior written permission. All inquiries should
be made to the publisher at the above address.

National Library of Australia Cataloguing-in-Publication Data:
Moore, David B.
    David Williamson's Jack Manning trilogy : a study guide.
    ISBN 0 86819 697 5.
    1. Williamson, David, 1942- – Criticism and interpretation. 2.
    Williamson, David, 1942- . Jack Manning trilogy. 3. Williamson,
    David, 1942- . Face to face. 4. Williamson, David, 1942- . A
    conversation. 5. Williamson, David, 1942- . Charitable intent. I.
    Title.
    A822.3

Book and cover design by Kate Florance, Currency Press.

Set by Currency Press in Caslon 540 BT

Printed by Ligare Book Printer, Riverwood

Contents

Acknowledgments

For their assistance with this project, thanks are due to: Victoria Chance and Deborah Franco at Currency Press; the playwright; directors, players and audience members from the Ensemble and La Mama premiere productions who kindly agreed to be interviewed; Merran Doyle at More Publicity, and the team at Anthony Williams Management. For their patience when this project was added to various others, special thanks to Emily, Eva and Joe.

Introduction

This book examines a trilogy of plays by Australia's foremost playwright, David Williamson. The plays, which premiered in Sydney and Melbourne between 1999 and 2001, deal with three different situations. The first play involves the staff of a commercial scaffolding firm. The second dramatises a meeting of two families affected by a brutal crime. The third involves the staff of a non-profit charitable organisation. Yet the basic format of each play is the same: there are no scene changes; the action unfolds in real time; all characters remain on stage throughout. The format is the same because all three plays dramatise the same 'Conferencing' process, following guidelines developed by a Sydney-based company, Transformative Justice Australia (TJA).

'Conferencing' provides a group of people in conflict with an opportunity to understand and acknowledge the specific sources of that conflict, so they can begin to transform conflict into cooperation.[1] *The Jack Manning Trilogy* is the result of an unusual collaboration between a playwright and professional Conferencing practitioners. David Williamson both observed Conferences and trained as a TJA Conference Convenor. He became intrigued by the Conferencing process and excited by its many potential applications. Each play was inspired, in part, by real-life case studies of TJA Conferences.

As a result, the plays have an unusual literary and dramatic form, and a strong socio-political intent. Unlike many Williamson plays, they are not primarily satires of existing institutions and sub-cultures. Rather, Williamson has dramatised a particular process. The Jack Manning plays demonstrate a powerful way of managing conflict constructively.

My position as author is also unusual. I have taught literature subjects and political science at universities, have an abiding interest in theatre, work with professional actors, and have been involved in administrative and legislative reforms involving Conferencing. These might be sufficient formal qualifications for commenting on David Williamson's trilogy.

However, I was also a founding Director of TJA, and continue to provide training for Conferencing Convenors internationally.[2] With my colleague John McDonald, I worked with David Williamson as he researched each of the three plays. John and I both commented on early drafts. So there is not the usual distance between author, critical commentator and subject matter. This lack of distance need not be a problem, but it is acknowledged in the interests of transparency.

Transparency happens to be one of three core principles guiding Convenors as we prepare for Conferences. The other two are clarity and respect.[3] The structure of this short text is designed to bring as much *clarity* as possible to the unusual elements of these plays: their minimalist literary–dramatic form and their campaigning socio-political content. The text provides a summary of the three plots, followed by an explanation of the theory and practice of Conferencing, and an examination of the origins of the trilogy.

The *Guide* also includes interviews with the playwright, with directors of the premiere productions, and with actors in those productions. David Williamson views his plays as 'blueprints for performance'.[4] While turning these blueprints into performances, directors and actors add insights and learn lessons along the way. Their insights and lessons become part of the play as performance. But the experiences of directors and actors can also add to our understanding of the 'play on the page'.

The 'architect' of the 'blueprint' and the builders are important, and so too are the people who live with the results. So the *Guide* also includes interviews with particular audience members, a group of people who share an experience of profound loss and who describe their responses to *A Conversation*. Again, their moving experience of the live performance enhances our understanding of the play.

The interviews are followed by a list of searching questions for further discussion and reflection, essential for any self-respecting study guide!

Finally, I would like to express *respect* for the reader who is sufficiently interested in these plays to study their important message in detail. The plays make for engaging and entertaining theatre, and that would be enough to warrant studying them closely. But the plays of *The Jack Manning Trilogy* also contribute to a broader social movement which aims to develop more constructive ways to manage the conflict that is an inevitable part of social life.

1. Plot summaries

Each play in *The Jack Manning Trilogy* portrays a Conference in real time. To summarise the plot of each play is to describe the dynamic of a Conference. And at a very general level, the Conference dynamic is the same in each play. The Convenor encourages participants to identify the basic facts and determine what caused or exacerbated the conflict and to describe how they have been affected. In a typical Conference, participants would then spend some time identifying how they can improve their situation.

The Conferences of the trilogy differ considerably from each other in this final stage. In *Face to Face*, participants formulate a detailed plan to move forward. In *A Conversation*, the two families are dealing with irreparable harm and their formal Conference agreement includes only one specific action. In this situation, as one bereaved father said in the wake of a real-life Conference, 'the process is the outcome'. Finally, in *Charitable Intent*, participants manage conflict by going their separate ways when the Conference makes it clear they are unable to work together.

Face to Face

In the first play of the trilogy, Conference Convenor Jack Manning brings together nine people associated with Baldoni's Exhibition Constructions, a scaffolding firm. Each of the nine has been affected in some way by a single dramatic incident and its aftermath. Glen Tregaskis, an employee at Baldoni's, assaulted the foreman, Richard Halligan and was summarily dismissed by owner/manager Greg Baldoni. Later that day, Glen drove to the Baldoni's house, waited in his car until Greg returned home, then 'rammed his bloody Mercedes' (p.6).[5]

The group have decided to convene a 'community Conference' rather than send Glen's case to the criminal justice system.[6] Glen attends with his mother, Maureen, and an old school friend, Barry. Greg Baldoni comes to the Conference with his wife Claire. Four other Baldoni's workers are there: Richard, the foreman; Luka, a scaffolder; Julie, Greg's personal assistant; and Therese, the company accountant.

Jack introduces all the participants, then invites Glen to recount how he came to ram Greg's car. Glen's overriding concern is to get his job back, a possibility that is not yet up for discussion. The participants have agreed to examine what happened and how each of them has been affected before considering how they might improve the situation.

Glen talks about the incident involving Greg's car and Jack invites him to consider how it affected Greg. Greg takes up the story, followed by Richard, then Claire. Each adds to the picture and raises new questions. Why, for instance, had Glen hit his foreman, Richard? After all, Richard had supported Glen more than anyone.

Gradually, a sorry tale of workplace intrigue unfolds. Glen has been the victim of a long-running and humiliating practical joke, in which women he fancies repeatedly stand him up. It turns out that Julie has played along. So has Luka. Even Therese was caught up in some of it. And Richard told Greg what was happening.

The first of several exchanges of apology and forgiveness follows these confessions. Glen apologises for hitting Richard. When Maureen accuses Richard of being weak for failing to protect Glen, Richard apologises.

Feeling put on the spot, Luka begins to explain his own motivations, and the scope of the discussion expands considerably. Luka and Greg argue vociferously about wages and conditions at Baldoni's. Luka accuses Richard of selling out his colleagues to gain a promotion. As it happened, the promotion never came. It turns out that Greg's son Adrian was given the job Richard wanted, and the discussion turns to family dynamics. This produces the revelation that Greg has been having an affair with his personal assistant, Julie.

This is this not Greg's first workplace affair either. We learn that he'd previously had an affair with Glen's mother, Maureen. Indeed, one of the reasons Greg stays at the Conference is his lingering sense of loyalty to Maureen. He wants to do the right thing by Maureen's son, despite the damage Glen has done to his car—and to his foreman. By staying in the Conference, Greg may help Glen avoid trial, and possibly jail. And so, despite his growing embarrassment and anger, Greg stays.

Julie feels compelled to explain why she became involved with Greg.

She describes a sense of existential despair. She, too, threatens to leave the Conference, and is persuaded to stay. Greg begins to show some vulnerability. At this point Jack reminds everyone of Claire's suggestion: they should examine the state of the workplace.

Luka explains his lack of motivation in words strikingly similar to Julie's. Richard admits his failings as a foreman, but confronts Greg about Baldoni's low wage rates. Jack seeks some objective financial facts from Therese. She confronts Greg with her sense of resentment and desperation about wages and conditions.

The issue of pay rates leads to broader questions about the way people communicate at Baldoni's, and how best to clarify people's roles and responsibilities. All the canvassed options seem feasible—other than giving Glen his job back. Glen's temper seems just too unpredictable. Barry, sensing his friend's growing desperation, explains some of the deeper reasons for Glen's behaviour.

With contributions from Glen and Maureen, Barry recounts a violent family history. One day Glen stood up to his father, Stan, who first threatened to murder Glen and Maureen, but suicided instead. Barry's story leaves people even more concerned about Glen's temper, especially when Barry is forced to reveal that when Glen felt humiliated on another occasion he threatened Barry himself with violence.

Jack speaks bluntly. Participants have to make a hard decision about Glen. Do they make it with their hearts or their heads? But instead of hearing an answer to the question, we hear another story of humiliation at Baldoni's. It's the story of Luka's humiliation at the hands of his colleagues. And Luka doesn't look for sympathy. Instead, he apologises immediately for his role in practical jokes at Glen's expense.

So now everyone at Baldoni's has admitted they could have acted differently—except Glen. Can he openly acknowledge that what he did was wrong? Can he learn to control his temper? Greg and Glen exchange apology and forgiveness. And this is a profound moment. It completes a circle. Everyone has now contributed to a fuller picture of what happened, and everyone has acknowledged that they might have done some things differently. They have all made themselves vulnerable.

At this point, Luka offers to take on the foreman's role, a role that would include responsibility for managing Glen. Luka's offer is accepted. The participants rapidly formulate an agreement. Claire articulates the key points, and Jack hastily records them.

The Conference participants now leave for drinks at the bar, while Jack formally writes up the agreement. He's interrupted for brief conversations, first with Maureen, then with Julie, and finally with Glen. Jack suggests that if Glen's about to lose his temper, he should think about how his mother will be affected. Glen, beer in hand, agrees that's great advice.

A Conversation

In *A Conversation*, Jack Manning brings together two families whose lives have been devastated by a crime. Derek and Barbara Milsom's daughter, Donna, was raped and murdered by Scott Williams. Scott's mother, Coral, has requested a Conference and brings her other son Mick, her daughter Gail, and her brother Bob. Lorin Zemanek, the psychologist who approved Scott's release on parole after an earlier sentence, also attends the Conference. Scott himself is now serving a life sentence in prison and cannot be there.

A Conversation opens with Lorin telling Jack that she's very sceptical about the Conferencing process. Derek and Barbara arrive and sound equally sceptical. When the Williams family arrives, Uncle Bob has no intention of staying. The tension is so great that Jack struggles to convince participants to take their seats.

Scott, we learn, has just been severely bashed by fellow inmates and is now in the prison hospital. Since Scott is not here in person, Jack has recorded him in prison (before he was bashed) and now plays the tape. In an eerily disembodied voice, Scott describes the prelude to his deadly assault. The scripted words lend themselves to delivery in an undramatic, factual tone, which heightens the brutality of Scott's description.

Jack begins to ask how people have been affected, but Coral immediately wants to talk about Scott's situation in protective custody. Coral is quick to point out that this was not why she requested the Conference. In fact Scott was bashed only last week, well after the Conference had been arranged. But the damage has been done: Derek and Barbara are enraged by the very hint that Coral might have an ulterior motive.

In their rage and despair, Derek and Barbara need little prompting to describe how they found out about Donna's death. Barbara describes her nightmares and the overwhelming distress that has ended her teaching career. Both feel their lives are over. So is their relationship—divorce is pending.

Their anger shifts to Lorin, the psychologist who approved Scott's release. But Scott's sister, Gail, wants to shift the focus away from Scott's psychology. She says that social factors strongly contributed to Scott's violent disregard for others.

Gail's family are quick to dismiss her 'factors'. Scott, they say, was born bad. To emphasise how bad, Derek reads from the Coroner's report. Its sickening details heighten Derek's fury and Barbara's distress.

Lorin pleads that what looks like professional failure was actually a *system* failure. The justice system failed to provide the levels of supervision she had recommended for Scott. The Williams family see a parallel in their own failures to supervise and reprimand Scott.

Derek and Lorin argue heatedly about the appropriate treatment of serial offenders. Derek insists that a character like Scott might respond to 'hard' behavioural deconditioning but Lorin's 'soft' 'talking cure' was bound to fail. Lorin threatens to leave. She stays only after Jack appeals to her sense of mutual professional respect.

Mick talks bitterly about a childhood shared with Scott. Uncle Bob defends the decision to sack Scott from his business after the first rape charge. Gail again urges Derek to accept that all these social factors influenced Scott. Derek pleads with Gail to return to reality, and to acknowledge that her brother is a profoundly damaged and dangerous man. But for the first time, Derek's tone is more distressed than angry.

Prompted by Derek's distress, Barbara pleads that the others still 'haven't *begun* to hear' (p.85). The murder robbed them not only of Donna's future; it also robbed them of her past. A common experience of pain links her with Coral, and Barbara's anger shifts to Derek who, she says, has failed to hear anyone else. Barbara addresses Coral and Gail as mother and daughter, and confesses that her own daughter had some less appealing characteristics.

Barbara explains that Donna's past has been stolen because the sequence in their photo album leads inexorably to the nightmare ending. Lorin suggests a practical response: why not shuffle the photos? Once everyone else seems to hear what she is saying, Barbara angrily accuses Derek of trying to control her grief.

Derek finally begins to talk personally. Once his anger shifts from

Lorin, she also makes a confession. Yes, intellectually she did understand Scott's situation. But she allowed herself to be charmed.

Mick confesses. In retrospect, he too could have tried harder with Scott. But down that path, he warns everyone, lies madness. Thousands of seemingly insignificant actions might have made the crucial difference. Bob wonders whether he might have inadvertently influenced Scott's predilection for violent sex. But nothing can bring Donna back.

Again, Mick cautions against too much introspection. He describes how the suicide of his best friend, Jimmy, has left Jimmy's father devastated. The story creates a connection between Derek and Mick. Even Derek now admits that he, too, could have done more to make Donna safe. He could have allowed Donna's boyfriend to move into her apartment; he could have arranged for a panic button.

So can anything practical be done? Coral again mentions a petition to have Scott placed in protective custody. A petition might influence the authorities. For her son it could mean the difference between life (in prison) and a violent death. Mick and Barbara agree: if only for Coral's sake, they don't want Scott dead. And Barbara agrees to sign. Derek will consider the matter. For now, he says, 'There's a weight of some kind been lifted' (p.103).

Charitable Intent

Bryony has been Chief Executive Officer of the charity Enabling and Caring for two-and-a-half years. The Board judged her predecessor to be likeable but ineffectual and appointed Bryony to reform the organisation. She seems to have the full support of three young executive assistants Cassie, Tamsyn and Giulia as well as the confidence of Board Chair, Brian, a successful businessman whose son has Down Syndrome. But other Board members are apparently less confident. Concerned by reports of conflict within the organisation, they have recommended a Conference, which Jack Manning convenes at E&C Headquarters. Brian, Bryony and the young executives attend alongside two long-standing E&C employees, Stella and Amanda.

Brian is concerned that Conferencing may be an inefficient process and, furthermore, that it might provide an opportunity for employer bashing. Jack first seats the participants, then responds. He provides his fullest explanation yet of the Conferencing process and its rationale. Brian remains sceptical. What if organisational conflict is not simply the result of misunderstandings and misperceptions? What if the conflict does have some objective basis? Jack points out that conflict is a problem for the organisation whether the sources are subjective or objective. The Conferencing process, he says, will help to clarify what is going on.

Jack starts the Conference with a chronological summary of key recent developments at E&C. His summary immediately exposes lines of conflict. Bryony and Giulia line up against Stella and Amanda. Brian agrees with Bryony that there is internal resistance to the new order.

The old guard certainly have grounds for resentment. Cassie has replaced Stella as financial controller; Giulia has replaced Amanda as head of public relations and marketing. Yet there are reasons to doubt that this is the whole story.

Bryony's new fundraising strategy, which involves television advertising and a direct phone appeal, ran into difficulties when Bryony dealt insensitively with a family whose child was demoted from the E&C advertising campaign. The child was distraught and the incident attracted damaging media coverage for E&C.

Stella asserts that Bryony's perpetual smile is a mask for anger. Brian supports his CEO. A leader, he says, should be respected, but if necessary also feared. Undaunted, Stella continues her attack. She damns Bryony's 'spy network' (p.121) and her profligate wining and dining of corporate donors. Stella then reveals that Bryony plans to star in a forthcoming series of E&C ads. Jack moves the conversation to the next major source of conflict.

Amanda was accused of poorly organising the gala ball, but the Board rejected Bryony's suggestion that she should be fired. As the story unfolds, Bryony gratuitously insults Giulia. The general tone turns more venomous and Bryony tries to limit what issues can be discussed. Jack overrides her on procedural grounds. And so does Brian. Brian's support for Bryony may be wavering.

The reason for Bryony's concern becomes clear as Amanda reveals more about Bryony's personal style. Tamsyn challenges the process, but Jack presses on. He examines exactly what Bryony has said to Amanda, and how she said it. Stella verifies Amanda's version of events. She explains how she urged Amanda to fight on.

Amanda and Bryony lock stares. Unexpectedly, Amanda wins. She describes how she took her concerns about Bryony's style to Tamsyn, but her confidence was betrayed and Bryony phoned her the following weekend and abused her. Bryony again seeks to divert the conversation. She appeals to Brian, but he rejects her appeal on procedural grounds, saying, 'We've started down this track' (p.137).

Amanda recounts how she was physically relocated. The system for overseeing branch offices was shifted from direct contact with colleagues to paper monitoring. After another tit-for-tat exchange between Amanda and Tamsyn, Jack asks Stella whether she feels she's been singled out. Stella takes the opportunity to reveal Bryony's '*new* new direction' (p.140). She's shifting the focus of the organisation from support for physically and mentally *disabled* children to support for socially *disadvantaged* children.

Now, for the first time, clear ideological differences emerge between Bryony and Brian. And while Bryony points the finger at Cassie and Giulia, there are unexpected signs of tension between Amanda and Stella. Amanda accuses Stella of enlisting her to fight Stella's personal fights.

Seemingly isolated, Amanda tells us that she has been diagnosed with breast cancer and describes how callously her colleagues received the news. But their attitude made her determined to fight even harder, and not to accept a severance package.

Suddenly, Brian offers a damning summary of problems with the whole executive. Without hesitation, Bryony abandons the rest of the team. They abandon her with equal speed, and an apparent surge of relief. Cassie and Tamsyn confess that Bryony's plotting reminds them of school bullying of the worst sort. Bryony offers an ultimatum: they go or she goes. Then she ups and goes.

Brian suggests to Cassie, Tamsyn and Giulia that their best available option at this early stage in their careers might be to seek alternative employment. They should go too. Brian thanks Jack. The situation has been clarified, as promised.

2. The theory and practice of Conferencing

Jack Manning appears in all three plays in essentially the same role: he is a professional Conference Convenor. Before we look at what that means, it's important to distinguish the Conferencing *process* from Conferencing *programs*. Briefly, the word 'program' concerns where Conferences are convened, by whom and for whom. What agency provides Conferencing, and what sort of cases does Conferencing deal with? The word 'process' is concerned with what actually happens once the Convenor brings the participants together. Who is asked what, and when are they asked?

The Jack Manning plays raise a number of questions about the *process* of Conferencing. These questions change in each play, partly because the three Conferences deal with different types of cases, and partly because each answer raises new questions. The playwright himself seems to start with two basic questions: 'How does Conferencing deal with matters that might normally be dealt with in a court?' and 'If people have a choice of processes, why wouldn't they just walk out of the emotionally more torrid one?'

Each play shows a different application of Conferencing. *Face to Face* portrays a Conference dealing with 'workplace issues' that could be categorised as 'crimes'. *Charitable Intent* is also set in the workplace, but it has no criminal justice element. Conversely, *A Conversation* focuses on the criminal justice applications of Conferencing and is not connected to the workplace. These differences in the application of Conferencing lead to different questions in each play about the process.

For instance, one of the key features of *A Conversation* is that the central character is not there. What is the point of convening a Conference if the perpetrator doesn't attend? Within the play the heated debate between Lorin and Derek about different modes of treatment addresses a related question: 'How does the collective process of Conferencing compare with therapeutic interventions for individuals?' Underlying these questions is that old favourite of the social sciences: 'How does Conferencing address the tension between free will and social determinism?'

Gail argues the case for socially-determined behaviour and her relentless talk of 'factors' acts as a catalyst. It brings to the surface an underlying conflict caused by differences in the participants' class, gender and ideology. This, in turn, heightens the conflict or tension between individuals who are members of opposing groups. In dramatising this conflict, the playwright asks: 'Do "structural tensions" between Conference participants make it more difficult for them to move beyond conflict and towards cooperation?'

A Conversation also raises issues about moral responsibility and free will. Some problems appear more complex the more closely one examines them. And with complex problems, a destructive outcome often derives not from one big failure, but from the steady accumulation of many small flaws and failures. But if this is the case, who can we blame for 'system failures'? If everybody has made just a small contribution along the way, does this mean that, ultimately, nobody is to blame for the final outcome?

Charitable Intent, focusing on the workplace, asks the opposite question: 'What if conflict really is caused by the actions of one person whose actions are vindictive and malicious?' Are we naïve if we assume that interpersonal conflict can always be transformed once people come to understand each other's points of view? In *Charitable Intent*, the views of one person seem quite incompatible with the views of everyone else. Once this has become clear, members of the affected community go their separate ways. The playwright seems to be asking: 'What is the point of convening a Conference when a community is actually disintegrating?'

Now all these questions are specifically about the *process* of Conferencing. There is an additional set of related questions about different *programs* that might use Conferencing.

In *Face to Face*, two of the incidents addressed in the Conference could have been dealt with in the criminal justice system. Glen has admitted he assaulted Richard and maliciously damaged Greg's car. But the incidents are dealt with in the workplace, and Conferencing is used as an *alternative* to court. If the process is successful, a court hearing becomes redundant.

In *A Conversation* the case has already been dealt with by the criminal justice system. Conferencing is an *adjunct* to court, rather than an alternative. It answers questions that the court cannot answer. Furthermore, this Conference seems to be a private affair, not part of some state-funded program. Barbara says to Coral that 'we'll share the cost' (p.102).

The issues of concern in *Charitable Intent* might have been taken before a tribunal under the aegis of the Anti-Discrimination Board, the Human Rights and Equal Opportunity Commission or the Industrial Relations Commission. As in *Face to Face*, however, the issues are addressed within the workplace. So again, Conferencing is offered as an *alternative*. And again, the play raises the *program* question of whether it is appropriate to address this sort of situation with Conferencing.

To answer all these questions, we need to understand in more detail just what Conferencing is. Only with a detailed understanding of the *process* can we adequately answer questions about *programs* that use Conferencing either as an alternative to some sort of tribunal, or as an adjunct.

What is Conferencing?

The following is a generic definition of Conferencing formulated by Transformative Justice Australia (TJA):

> A process in which a group of people affected by conflict are brought together to consider:
> i.   what happened,
> ii. how they have been affected, and
> iii. what can be done to improve their situation.

Einstein once suggested that everything should be as simple as possible, but no simpler. We reached this simple-as-possible definition of Conferencing after nearly a decade of work. We experimented; we made adjustments; we formulated and distilled a theory that explained what we were doing. A brief overview of developments through the 1990s helps explain this further.

The first legislation providing for some form of Conferencing in the justice system was passed in the New Zealand parliament in 1989. *The*

Children, Young Persons and their Families Act provided for a process called 'family group conferencing', which was to be used for both 'youth justice' and for 'care and protection' matters. In cases where a person between the ages of ten and eighteen had committed a crime, and also in cases where a young person might need alternative living arrangements, a convenor from the Department of Social Welfare could bring the affected parties together and help them try to reach an agreement.[7]

More than a decade later, the primary significance of the New Zealand legislation is that it reflected a shift in thinking about the way the state should deal with social problems. The 1989 legislation viewed people less as the passive recipients of punishment or services from state agencies, and more as citizens who could be supported to find ways to deal with their own problems. Observers were impressed to see this democratic philosophy translated into national legislation.

Not surprisingly, the New Zealand legislation soon raised interest in Australia. In 1990, a delegation of four observers from New South Wales travelled to New Zealand to examine its practical effects. The delegation included John McDonald, a former teacher who had been appointed Principal Adviser on Youth Affairs to reforming NSW Police Commissioner John Avery. John McDonald was impressed by much of what he saw in New Zealand. In a paper entitled *Can it be done another way?*, he argued that police and other justice system agencies in New South Wales could deal with young people far more efficiently, effectively and fairly.

Police in New South Wales were already entitled to exercise discretion in a large range of cases involving young people who admitted committing the offence in question. Except for very serious ('indictable') offences, a police Sergeant could divert a case from court and instead issue a formal warning to the offender(s) about the consequences of further lawbreaking.

Yet many police were sceptical about the value of diverting cases from court and the proportion of diverted cases varied considerably from one district to another. John McDonald believed that police might divert many more cases if there were truly effective alternatives. He suggested offering some form of Conferencing in the legal space occupied by formal police cautioning so that, in the aftermath of a crime, police could help a community of people to turn a problem into an opportunity. Commissioner Avery was prepared to say, 'Make it happen!' but it took a year or so to find a group of people with the right mix of enthusiasm, expertise and distance from Sydney.

In 1991, at the invitation of local police, John outlined his proposal to a group of professionals in the southern New South Wales city of Wagga Wagga. I attended that meeting as Coordinator of Justice Studies at Charles Sturt University. A group of us then worked with the city's community police unit to establish a program of 'Effective Cautioning using Family Group Conferencing'.[8]

This program very quickly reduced the proportion of youth justice cases being sent to the local court. More importantly, cases diverted to Conferencing seemed to achieve more positive outcomes than comparable cases sent to court. Conferencing (i) delivered very high rates of participant satisfaction, while apparently (ii) lowering rates of re-offending, and (iii) increasing the quality and quantity of relationships in each affected community.[9] These three statistical outcomes from the Conferencing *program* seemed to be interrelated. There seemed to be less conflict and stronger social support in each affected community. There was less disengagement and/or less destructive engagement. There was more constructive engagement. In other words, people were finding an alternative to avoiding each other or arguing unproductively with each other. An intense conversation about the sources of their conflict was helping them find a third way beyond 'flight or fight'.

Not surprisingly, we were particularly interested in the *process* that was delivering these outcomes. We had begun with the simple idea of bringing together a group of people affected by the one incident. We had a general strategy, but we lacked specific tactics:

◆ Who should attend?
◆ Who should be asked to speak first?
◆ What exactly should they be asked?
◆ What were the guiding principles?

We did not realise at the time what a long and complicated journey these questions would take us on. Through the three or four years that the original Conferencing program ran in Wagga, a group of us examined the process in detail. We sought to formulate the ideal wording for the questions that a Conference Convenor should ask participants. We sought to determine an optimal sequence in which to ask those questions. And we asked many other questions:

◆ What were the criteria for including or excluding certain participants?
◆ Was there an optimal number of participants?
◆ What sorts of outcomes were desirable, and why?

To answer these questions, we drew on a wide range of disciplines, including political philosophy, social theory, linguistics and psychology. One aspect of the process that was particularly intriguing was how there seemed to be a common emotional pattern in Conferences. It took us quite some time to articulate what was occurring, but as Conference participants painted a picture of what had happened and how each of them had been affected, the collective emotional tone shifted. Put simply, the degree of anger, fear and contempt in the room seemed to subside.

Perhaps more significantly, this shift away from the most negative emotions seemed to involve some sort of emotional 'contagion' or 'resonance'. A sense of common feeling grew as the Conference proceeded. Participants acknowledged the source(s) of conflict among themselves. As they did so, they seemed to express emotions less as lone individuals and more as members of a group. And emotions fed off each other. When one or two people became visibly less angry, more surprised or more interested, others followed.

We explained this phenomenon in terms of a universal human ability to communicate directly and powerfully through 'basic emotions' or affects. Since that time, a growing number of researchers have turned their attention to similar group phenomena. They have examined the sociology of 'group emotion' in workplaces. They have studied the physiology of 'interpersonal limbic regulation'.[10] In other words, they have asked how the limbic system—those areas of the brain most involved with emotions—not only influences our *internal* thoughts and feelings, but also influences our *external* relationships, and so influences the dynamics of groups. This area of theory has remained invaluable as we have worked to improve Conferencing, and to design other processes for managing conflict.[11]

As we were seeking to understand the Conferencing *process* better, we were also engaged by external critics in a debate about the *program*. Their key question was whether or not Conferencing in the justice system should be coordinated by police. The debate was often confused. Strongly held views on the pros and cons of the Conferencing *process* were too frequently conflated with the separate question of whether police should coordinate a Conferencing *program*.

In New South Wales, the debate about program design for Conferencing in youth justice was resolved in 1997. New legislation created a Directorate to coordinate 'Youth Justice Conferencing' (YJC) through the NSW Department of Juvenile Justice (DJJ). The YJC Directorate now oversees a statewide network of Administrators, one in each of seventeen districts. The Administrators, in turn, coordinate a group of YJC Convenors who prepare and convene youth justice Conferences.

The Youth Justice Conference Convenors are carefully selected, then trained in legal and administrative aspects of the program, and in the process of Conferencing. Rather than being full-time employees of the Department of Juvenile Justice, the Convenors are local residents from a range of professional and social backgrounds, who sub-contract to the Department for each Conference they convene. This arrangement centralises those elements that are best centralised, while engaging local residents in positive social control. This sounds good in theory and, fortunately, the legislation also seems to be working well in practice.[12]

By the time this legislation was passed, our understanding of Conferencing had developed considerably. In 1995, John McDonald and I established Transformative Justice Australia (TJA) with John's brother, industrial relations lawyer Mark McDonald. Our dual goal was to improve training for Conference Convenors, and to offer Conferencing to organisations as a conflict management service.

We had already used Conferencing to manage tensions between staff in the justice system. We were also trialling the process in schools on Queensland's Sunshine Coast and again saw the potential to use Conferencing to deal with staff conflict. It seemed increasingly obvious that the process could be used more widely in workplaces. But police and teachers had been offered Conferencing free of charge in our pilot programs. Why should a government department or a private company pay someone to facilitate a Conference? To enunciate the commercial value of the Conferencing process, we were compelled to rethink the underlying principles and the design of the process as well as the language used to explain it.

Conferencing in the justice system was generally described as a meeting 'between offender(s), victim(s), and their supporters'. This terminology was inappropriate in schools and it was also not right for most applications of Conferencing in commercial workplaces.

For a start, most workplace conflict isn't associated with any single incident. Typically it develops over time, and many of the incidents along the way have no obvious 'victim' or 'offender'. Rather, unresolved misunderstandings leave people resentful and mistrustful. Gradually, colleagues and friends become embroiled. When two colleagues fall out, everyone around them has three options: side with one, side with the other, or 'stay out of it'. Sadly, each of these options eventually makes the situation worse. Only some sort of collective response can address collective conflict.

Furthermore, pre-existing conflicts between groups often also play out in a workplace. Two people may mistrust each other because they identify with different ethnic groups that happen to be feuding. The major harm and suffering occurred at some distant time in another place. There may be no clear-cut victims and offenders in the present.

In short, bringing together victims and offenders in the justice system was just one of several possible applications of Conferencing. Defining the process in terms of victims and offenders confused a broadly applicable *process* with its narrow application in one particular *program*. In order to apply Conferencing successfully elsewhere, we needed to identify what was common to *all* the situations for which Conferencing was suitable. Another debate around this time helped us to do this.

Alternative Dispute Resolution

From the outset, Conferencing was frequently categorised as a form of 'mediation'. The idea that a third party can help people to resolve their differences somewhere other than a court or tribunal is increasingly on the rise. Professional mediators work in industrial relations, in other areas of law, and in community mediation programs. Many schools have introduced 'peer mediation'. These approaches are also categorised as 'Alternative Dispute Resolution' (ADR).

People are seeking *alternatives* more and more because courts and other tribunals are costly, both in money and time. So court seems *inefficient*. More problematically, for certain types of case, court also seems *ineffective*. In short, people involved in a court case can be unhappy with the *outcome* and the *process* by which that outcome was reached.

This is not to denigrate the courts. The adversarial court process plays a very important role. It seeks a single version of the truth, which is presented in the form of the judge's decision and formally resolves a dispute. However, this dispute resolution is sometimes achieved at significant personal cost to those involved because the process maximises the conflict between disputants.

The best-known ADR processes are mediation, conciliation and arbitration. These differ mainly in the degree to which the third party facilitator contributes to the agreement, and the extent to which that agreement is legally binding. Mediation is considered the least coercive of the three processes, and the one in which disputing parties have the greatest degree of control. Mediation offers to *minimise conflict* while resolving the dispute(s).

The word *mediation* can be confusing because it has come to have two distinct meanings, one broad, one narrow. In broad terms 'mediation' describes the general *category* of processes in which a third party assists people to resolve disputes in a non-adversarial manner. In this usage, the word 'mediation' and the phrase 'Alternative Dispute Resolution' have much the same meaning. If the word 'mediation' refers to a *category* of processes where a third party assists people to deal with difficult issues, then Conferencing can be said to be a form of mediation.

But the more common definition of 'mediation' is narrower and refers to just one *process* within the broader category of ADR processes. 'Interest-based mediation', as it is sometimes called, is a process in which the third party *assists a negotiation*. Members of Harvard University's Negotiation Project, in their widely influential *Getting to Yes*, identified its core principles as follows:

> The mediator assists the negotiation by having those involved:
> ◆ separate the people from the problem;
> ◆ focus on interests, not positions;
> ◆ invent options for mutual gain; and
> ◆ insist on the use of objective criteria.[13]

These principles encourage participants to agree on as much as possible, and then agree to disagree on what remains. Yet most people who are trained in interest-based mediation and who have some professional mediating experience will agree that mediation 'doesn't always work'. In some cases, it can be difficult to find *any* common ground between the parties and interest-based mediation is not always the most suitable process to deal with the situation at hand. Yet we found that mediators sometimes struggled to determine when mediation was appropriate. *The common problem seemed to be the lack of an adequate tool to diagnose situations of conflict.*

Managing Conflict

Many situations are diagnosed as 'disputes' when in fact there is *no* dispute. Other situations involve *many* disputes, which are mostly symptoms of deeper interpersonal conflict. It is conflict that makes the situation problematic.

This distinction ought to have been clear to us from our very early days in Wagga. Cases were only considered eligible for Conferencing if the accused young person or people had admitted their involvement. In other words, there had to be *no dispute* about the basic facts of the matter. And if there was no dispute, then *dispute resolution*, whether with an adversarial or non-adversarial *process*, was redundant.

Victims of crime were awake to this distinction. 'What is there to *mediate?*' was a common response if we used the word 'mediation' instead of 'Conferencing'. What was required was not, in the first instance, that two parties *negotiate* an agreement for the future. Rather, *all* the people affected needed an opportunity to paint a detailed picture of the past and the present. Only then could they look collectively to the future.

To articulate this distinction between Conferencing and interest-based mediation we needed to distinguish disputes from conflict. We examined current popular usage of the words 'dispute' and 'conflict' among English speakers in various countries. We examined formal definitions and etymology. Sure enough, the difference between a dispute and a conflict is clear and widely understood. It is a difference in *kind*, not just degree.

> A *dispute* is a contest over a specific set of *facts*. It requires two parties, but need not involve negative feelings between them. On the other hand, interpersonal *conflict* is a state, arising from some sort of opposition, in which those affected experience negative *feelings* about one another.[14]

People in conflict:

- ◆ identify other people as the problem;
- ◆ cling to their own fixed positions;
- ◆ see no possibility of mutual gain, feeling they can only win if the others lose;
- ◆ insist on their own subjective criteria.

By definition, then, the emotions associated with conflict compel people in conflict to breach all the basic rules for negotiation. People in conflict cannot *engage constructively* until they have acknowledged the sources of that conflict, and until they have begun to transform conflict into cooperation. Then they might begin to negotiate—if there is, indeed, anything to negotiate. There may not be.

In short, the single most significant difference between the *processes* of interest-based *mediation* and *Conferencing* is that mediation is generally unsuitable when people are in significant conflict, whereas Conferencing is designed expressly to deal with this. Conferencing creates the circumstances in which the sources of conflict can be acknowledged, and the *conflict can begin to be transformed*. Conference participants can move away from anger, fear and contempt, towards interest and relief.

By distinguishing between disputes and conflicts, we identified three general approaches to conflict management:

◆ *maximising* conflict—an unfortunate side-effect of adversarial dispute resolution processes;

◆ *minimising* conflict—a deliberate negotiating tactic for non-adversarial dispute resolution, which works if those involved are prepared to seek agreement on as much as possible, and agree to disagree on the rest;

◆ *transforming* conflict—an appropriate tactic where conflict has become more significant to those involved than have the details of any particular dispute.

These distinctions make it easier to choose the right conflict management process. If someone is *accused* of doing something that, by policy or law, must be dealt with formally, and if the accused *clearly disputes* that accusation, then the appropriate process is *adjudication*. A likely side effect of the adjudication, however, will be to maximise conflict between those involved.

If a *dispute* seems to have arisen from *lack of clarity* about the issues, and if the dispute seems to affect *only two parties*, then interest-based *mediation* or assisted negotiation may be appropriate. A mediator can manage any minor existing conflict, and can *minimise* the emergence of new conflict. Other processes are available for *disputes* affecting *more than two parties*. However, if there is significant conflict, then conflict *transformation* is required.

The causes and consequences of conflict fall into three general categories. Conflict may:

◆ arise from an *undisputed* and *harmful* act, and/or

◆ be associated with *many* poorly resolved *disputes* between *individuals*, and/or

◆ be a legacy of poorly resolved *disputes* between *groups*.

These situations are not mutually exclusive. Conferencing is suitable for addressing all of them.

TJA Conferencing

Conferencing in the justice system is typically used for cases where the accused has confessed to involvement in the crime, which is to say, for cases of *undisputed harm*. Early versions of the process, used for care and protection and for youth justice matters, were called 'family group conferencing', a phrase now used largely for Conferencing in 'community-centred child and welfare practice'.[15] In justice systems, the process was labelled 'family conferencing' or 'group conferencing' and is now frequently linked with a North American–based reform movement, known as 'restorative justice conferencing'.[16]

From 1995, when we established TJA, we ran training workshops for Conference Convenors in Australia and North America. Because of our experience convening Conferences in Australian workplaces, we favoured the term 'community conferencing', emphasising that the 'community' in question was very specific. In justice system applications, it was the 'community of people affected by the crime'. In workplace applications of Conferencing, it was the community of people who worked in the same organisation, although the conflict itself was typically associated with *many* poorly resolved *disputes* between individuals. Accordingly, we began to differentiate these applications of Conferencing with the twin terms 'community conferencing' and 'workplace conferencing'.

Yet there were two problems with this terminology. First, we had worked hard to develop a single generic process that could be applied in many different programs. The use of separate terms obscured this distinction between one process and many programs. Second, several commercial and government organisations made use of our training materials and terminology, but their derivative trainings produced varying styles of facilitation. What others were calling 'community conferencing' differed significantly from what we understood by the term.

We wanted to separate ourselves from these training programs because they tended to disregard or distort the guiding principles we had developed. For instance, some Conferencing training programs reduced Conference facilitation to rote-learned procedure. Convenors were told to follow verbatim a set of scripted questions. Inevitably,

Convenors trained in this way were not prepared to handle unexpected situations. We saw this as unfair both to the Convenors and to their Conference participants.

We believe that clearly articulated guiding principles are required to prevent facilitation from being reduced to unthinking procedure. For instance, we understand Conferencing to be a *deliberative democratic* process, in which people directly affected by an issue make decisions about that issue in a manner that seems as fair as possible. To maximise the sense of fairness for all participants, a Convenor needs to adhere to principles of participation, equity, deliberation and non-tyranny.[16] That is to say, all those affected should have the opportunity to participate; they should participate as equals; their suggestions should be acknowledged and deliberated. And no participant should stop another from participating as an equal, and having suggestions acknowledged and deliberated.

Importantly, a Convenor must achieve non-tyranny in a non-tyrannical way. For instance, it would be easy enough to pass laws compelling people to participate in Conferencing programs and to reach certain outcomes. Indeed, politicians in various countries have understood Conferencing in the justice system this way. In both the United Kingdom and Australia, for instance, politicians have declared that offenders will be forced to apologise to victims. But forcing apologies is a form of tyranny. It is not Conferencing as we know it.

Furthermore, a Convenor might formally prohibit certain behaviours, stopping participants from speaking angry words or using intimidating body language. And indeed, some dispute resolution processes do attempt to minimise conflict by imposing these sorts of 'ground rules' on behaviour. Rules of this nature can foster superficially polite words and tone, but they do so at significant cost. Behavioural prohibitions can stop the causes and consequences of conflict from being acknowledged.

An alternative approach to managing conflict in a small group involves:

◆ expanding the circle, ensuring that all the participants who ought to participate are indeed there;

◆ ensuring that participants understand and accept the formal structure of the Conference, which guarantees that issues are dealt with in chronological sequence, with an initial emphasis on specific actions; and

◆ paying very careful attention to all aspects of the Convenor's communication, such that the Convenor is not drawn into the conflict, and sets a baseline mood of concerned but calm interest.

The Convenor follows a standard sequence, addressing the person who acted first in whatever scene is being revisited. That person is invited to describe what happened, step by step, so that a picture is painted in everyone's mind's eye. The person most immediately affected is asked next, followed by other people who have been affected. Gradually, a picture emerges of how conflict has spread through a social network, like ripples on a pond.

As participants collectively 'paint a picture' of what happened, the mood shifts. A Convenor learns to recognise this underlying affective sequence, allowing it to happen without becoming overly caught up in the prevailing mood. The Convenor monitors this collective mood. As the conversation moves through the standard Conference sequence, the mood is transformed from conflict to cooperation.

As our understanding of the process evolved, so did our terminology. By 2001 we adopted the simplest terminology for 'the generic process of Conferencing as developed and practised by TJA and applicable in community-, government- and/or corporate sectors', namely 'TJA Conferencing'. A 'conflict management matrix' explained Conferencing as just one of several processes that could be used to cut the costs of conflict in organisations. (See pages 23.) A clearer understanding of the Conferencing process allows us now to ask a set of 'process' questions about the plays.

How realistic are these plays?

Conferencing has certainly been used to deal effectively with the types of matters dramatised in *The Jack Manning Trilogy*. It's true that the plays don't last as long as 'the real thing', and they don't involve as many participants. A typical Conference dealing with matters of this complexity and seriousness might last five hours, or even longer. Around twelve to fifteen people would typically attend. Nevertheless, to those of us who have participated in and/or convened a Conference, the plays feel startlingly realistic. They seem neither less complex nor shorter than 'the real thing'.

This sense that the plays are the right length and involve the right numbers of participants has something to do with the difference between

Workplace Conflict Management Matrix

SITUATION	DESCRIPTION	OPTIMAL PROCESS	THE THIRD PARTY
An *accusation* which is *clearly disputed*, and which must, by law and/or administrative guidelines, be dealt with formally.	Clearly disputed accusation	**Formal fact-finding**	Gathers and reviews evidence, then *resolves the dispute* by imposing a judgement.
A *dispute* arising from *lack of clarity* about the issues, and affecting *two key parties*.	Dispute between two parties	**Assisted negotiation**	*Helps disputants resolve their dispute* by clarifying/reframing issues and so distinguishing: ◆ people from problems; ◆ where people want to be from how to get there; ◆ optimal ways of getting there.
Disputes arising from *lack of clarity* about various issues, and involving *more than two parties*.	Disputes between several parties	**Dialogue with solutions**	*Structures out conflict and structures in cooperation* with a meeting format that identifies in sequence: ◆ general experiences; ◆ specific problems; ◆ optional solutions.
Significant *conflict* associated with: ◆ a *harmful* act about which there is *no dispute*; and/or ◆ *many* poorly resolved disputes between *individuals*; and/or *groups*.	Specific conflict with *no dispute or many disputes*	**Conferencing**	Brings together everyone affected and *helps participants transform conflict into cooperation* by considering: ◆ what happened; ◆ how people have been affected; ◆ how best to improve the situation.
General conflict between individuals and groups within a medium/large organisation or other community.	General conflict in a large organisation	**Constructive communication workshop**	Prepares and convenes a workshop where colleagues *identify styles and systems of communication conducive to cooperation*, then develop a plan for turning theory into practice.

participating in a Conference and observing one. The degree of emotional intensity is much greater for people inside the circle. As those directly affected focus intently on urgent issues, every detail of which is significant to them, time seems to travel unusually quickly. For an audience of outsiders, however, the playwright can edit out extraneous details, highlight key issues and accentuate the turning points of the Conference.

Is this how these matters would unfold?

The short answer is yes. Indeed, the first performance of *Face to Face* was a revelation to those of us familiar with some of the real cases that had helped to inspire the play. The Conference seemed extraordinarily realistic, despite its shorter duration and smaller participant numbers, and also despite the fact that Jack says and does some things that a Convenor would typically avoid.

Jack breaches a few of the guidelines designed to ensure that Conference Convenors are perceived as neutral. For instance, he asks closed questions (that can be answered with a simple 'yes' or 'no'), rather than open questions that encourage an expansive response. He alludes to facts that people have revealed to him in private. On more than one occasion he can't resist being baited. In frustration, he says things that would be better said by others. He's less than subtle when participants threaten to leave. Convenors are trained to resist all these temptations in a Conference, to avoid any hint that the Convenor is taking sides and favouring some participants.

Again, however, these variations don't seem to detract from the realism of the plays. In effect, the playwright externalises some of Jack's internal drama. His occasional frustration and annoyance become visible, especially in *Face to Face*. He reveals some of his personal opinions, especially in *Charitable Intent*. The audience is allowed to glimpse the character behind an otherwise studiously neutral façade.

How does Jack Manning compare to a standard TJA convenor?

Generally, Jack follows the standard sequence provided for in the TJA Conferencing script. The script consists of a set of optional questions to each participant according to their role in the conflict and the nature of the case. Thus, Conference participants may revisit just one incident (as is typical in criminal justice cases), or they may revisit three or four incidents (as is typical in workplaces and other communities).

Either way, Jack starts by questioning the *person or people who acted first*. The script prompts that person to paint a detailed picture of what actually happened, in what context and with what motivation. The next prompt is for the *person or people most directly affected*, followed by the *people accompanying them* and, finally, *people accompanying the person who acted first*. A detailed picture gradually emerges. As it does, the collective sense grows that 'we are all in the same boat'. Only then is it appropriate to ask 'Now what do we do about all this?' In *A Conversation*, that question becomes 'Is there anything else anyone would like to say?' In *Charitable Intent*, Jack offers a wryly understated observation, rather than a question: 'Brian, I've got the feeling you've got a bit off a problem here' (p.149).

The understatement is less an expression of Jack's character and more a studied general posture that Convenors are strongly urged to adopt during the Conference. A significant component of Convenor training is to practise a paradoxical stance we have called, variously 'empathic impartiality' and 'detached engagement'. The aim is to achieve a tone of voice, bodily posture and, most visibly, facial expressions that convey this general message of a concerned referee.

The facial expression that most conveys 'detached engagement' is a combination of distress and interest, both displayed equally mildly. The general message this sends is: 'I'm interested in what you have to say, although the situation is upsetting. I'll listen with concern, though I won't take sides'. But as the Convenor asks each question, there's a more specific message, something like: 'Help us out, here. If you respond adequately to my open question, I'll remain interested. If you don't offer an adequate response, I'll become more distressed'. The look alone is often enough to encourage open, honest storytelling.

What are the dramatic reasons for diverging from the standard?

Jack bends the rules for convening a Conference only slightly in each play. Importantly, he bends the rules differently in each case. David Williamson has done this for philosophical and dramatic reasons. As we have seen, in each play Williamson asks—and answers—a different set of questions about the Conferencing process and its applications.

Face to Face was completed two years before *A Conversation* and *Charitable Intent*. As the first play of the trilogy, it addresses general questions about the inner drama of a Convenor. In the most heated moments of the play, some of Jack's inner drama becomes external. Most obviously, along with other participants, Jack begins to lose patience with Glen, cajoling him, and even momentarily becoming sarcastic. Yet what brings Glen to his senses is not Jack's heated tone and actions. Rather, Glen is ultimately overwhelmed by the vulnerability and the support of others.

In 'real life', Jack could almost certainly have achieved this outcome simply by looking—intently!—at the right people at the right time, and asking them the right questions. By becoming visibly frustrated and angry as he does in *Face to Face*, Jack runs the risk that he will be seen as partisan instead of a neutral referee. The playwright alerts us to this risk by having Barry warn Glen not to trust Jack, because 'he just sits in the middle'. But that is precisely why Jack is trustworthy. By remaining loyal to the process, rather than supporting any one individual, the Convenor helps achieve the optimal outcome for everyone.

There is a trade-off here. Jack certainly risks being seen as partisan when he shows his frustration. This is not a problem for the play. On the contrary, the audience is startled when Jack loses his cool and the moment is *dramatically* very effective. It may have been a dramatic risk for Williamson had he *not* allowed Jack to raise his voice and leave his seat. But *philosophically* Jack's words and deeds misrepresent the Convenor's technique and the nature of the Conferencing process. It's possible the audience could take Jack's words and deeds as an accurate portrayal of standard Convenor's technique. In the event this did not seem to happen. Time and again after performances of the Ensemble production of *Face to Face*, for instance, audience members interested in Jack's technique were able to locate exactly where dramatic licence had been used to make visible Jack's inner drama.

In contrast, Jack remains studiously neutral in *A Conversation*. Indeed Geoff Cartwright observes that for the actor playing the Convenor, *A Conversation* is less engaging than *Face to Face*. There is little if any tension between Jack and the two participating families in *A Conversation*. Jack clearly expects the Conference to be emotionally intense and demanding, but the main sources of conflict are external: one is political, the other professional.

The political conflict concerns the general approach to 'law and order' matters, and even more generally, the philosophical justification for revenge or retribution. There are several allusions to the politics of law and order through the play. Perhaps the most succinct example is Jack's injunction, before the Conference proper begins, that there must be no violence. This is like the command 'Don't think of a white elephant'— which immediately brings the creature to mind. In a real Conference, the Convenor would safeguard against violence in various subtler but more effective ways. Yet the play is more dramatically effective because Jack brings the possibility of violence to the fore.

More overtly dramatic is the professional tension between Jack and the psychologist Lorin. She expresses scepticism, not only about the worth of Conferencing, but also about certain modes of treatment for offenders with Scott's profile. When Derek, in his rage, makes a strong case against Lorin's professional practice, there is a risk that Jack will be seen as allied with Derek, against Lorin.

In short, when Jack bends the rules for convening a Conference in *Face to Face*, he dramatises his own internal conflict. In *A Conversation*, we see little of Jack's internal conflict but we sense conflict in two other arenas as the Conferencing process challenges both the political philosophy of the justice system and some professional practices in clinical psychology. Jack bends the rules in *Charitable Intent*, in yet a different way. By taking a slightly partisan position before the Conference is over, Jack is displaying neither personal nor professional conflict. Rather, he is adding his voice to a conflict of ideas, big debates about different philosophies of government, business and social welfare. In this way, Jack highlights a major 'structural conflict' between institutions, ideas and groups.

A second major source of interpersonal conflict in *Charitable Intent* derives from Bryony herself. A combination of temperament and experience which has produced in Bryony a personality brimming with contempt for pretty much everybody. Bryony's contempt probably extends to Jack, but he remains disciplined, as a skilled Convenor must, in Bryony's presence. Only after she leaves the Conference does Jack allow himself to comment on the damage she has caused with her abrasive, manipulative manner.

How would these matters be referred to a Conference?

The way these matters would be referred to a Conference is an interesting question, with different and evolving answers for each play. The NSW Attorney General's Department has mooted the idea of diverting cases in the adult criminal justice system from the courts to Conferencing. However, the state government had not passed any legislation to this effect at the time of writing. In *Face to Face* Conferencing would not be an option if Glen's case reached the criminal justice system. Rather, in the play, those associated with the incidents at Baldoni's effectively conspire to keep the whole affair from entering 'the system'. So Glen's actions remain in a moral grey zone. If his colleagues, family and friends can find an acceptable and workable response, then everything that Glen has done—and everything that prompted him to do it—will remain classified as 'workplace relations'. Each of the participants in the Conference is walking a moral and legal tightrope. Together, they manage not to fall.

As of 2001, the case dramatised in *A Conversation* could be dealt with in a Conference as part of an official program in New South Wales run by the Restorative Justice Unit of the Department of Corrections. New Zealand has a similar program. Both jurisdictions established Conferencing programs for serious criminal matters in the same year that *A Conversation* premiered at the Ensemble Theatre. Indeed, the Minister for Corrections officially declared the New South Wales program permanent during the Ensemble season.

The key difference between most current official Conferencing programs and Conferencing for very serious criminal matters is that most programs currently use the process as an *alternative* to traditional processes rather than an *adjunct*. Williamson portrays a Conference convened as an *unofficial* adjunct to the workings of the criminal justice system.

There are a growing number of programs, particularly in North America, that similarly offer some sort of unofficial or semi-official adjunct to 'the system'. Many of these programs claim to offer a 'restorative' alternative to the 'retributive' official response. Faith-based, university-, or government-funded community agencies typically administer these programs, and most use a process known as 'victim-offender mediation' or 'victim-offender reconciliation'. A handful of programs have begun explicitly to use Conferencing, with its stronger emphasis on the whole group, and its capacity to handle intense conflict constructively. If, as we hope, various programs are adequately evaluated, and there is constructive dialogue between practitioners and policy-makers, it is likely that Conferencing will be offered more widely to people whose lives have been strongly affected by crime.

The Enabling and Caring matter portrayed in *Charitable Intent* could be referred to Conferencing quite simply. TJA made Conferencing available to organisations as a conflict management process from 1995. It was used almost exclusively in Sydney and the Illawarra until 2001, after which various large organisations began also to 'deploy' us interstate and even overseas.

In *Charitable Intent*, at least one member of the board is familiar with Conferencing, and has recommended the process to the board. Brian, who was sceptical about the worth of the exercise, was outvoted. There's some irony, then, that Brian's outlook is the one most affected by the Conference, which reveals to him the modus operandi of his protégée Bryony.

3. Genesis of the trilogy

I have described in the introduction to the published plays how David Williamson became interested in the theory and practice of Conferencing.[18] The timing was significant. In April 1998 the Sydney Theatre Company was staging a production of Williamson's strongly autobiographical play, *After the Ball*, at the Opera House. *After the Ball* seemed to break a long-running pattern in Williamson's writing for the stage. Biographer Brian Kiernan has observed that, from the start of Williamson's career, the subject of his plays has alternated regularly between institutions and individuals.[19] But the subject of *After the Ball* is both the *institution* of the family in general, and the intensely characterised *individual* members of a family strikingly similar to Williamson's own.

A period of frenetic productivity followed *After the Ball*. Rather than alternating his focus from institutions to individuals, Williamson now wrote two different types of play in parallel. From 1999 through 2001, he continued a successful tradition of premiering productions with the Sydney Theatre Company. The subject of each play is an 'institution' of sorts: the architectural profession of *Corporate Vibes* (1999), the Labor Party in *The Great Man* (2000), the Sydney art world of *Up For Grabs* (2001), and the milieu of Australian literature and literary criticism portrayed in *Soulmates* (2002). The style is satirical social comedy, or comedy of manners.

Meanwhile, *The Jack Manning Trilogy* plays were premiered at the Ensemble and La Mama. Their subject is neither an institution nor an individual. Rather, the subject of the trilogy is a philosophy and a process. And though the style of the plays seems closer to drama than comedy, there are certainly some genuinely comic moments.

In retrospect, then, *After the Ball* marks a watershed in Williamson's career. His plays moved beyond a dichotomy of individuals and institutions. They perhaps also moved beyond the traditional dichotomy of social comedy and drama. Surrogacy, observed the playwright about his 2003 play *Birthrights*, 'requires a solemn approach, though not without humour'. Appropriately, Williamson offered premiere production rights for *Birthrights* to *The Jack Manning Trilogy* directors, Sandra Bates in Sydney and Tom Gutteridge in Melbourne.[20]

While *After the Ball* was playing at the Opera House, Williamson wrote a review article in the 'Australian Review of Books', a monthly supplement to the *Australian* newspaper. The article, 'Mixed Feelings', reviewed *What Emotions Really Are* by Sydney University–based philosopher Paul Griffiths.[21] Williamson argued that the discipline of psychology should seek common ground with other biological and social sciences, rather than continuing to debate the merits of two exaggerated doctrines. One of these doctrines emphasised universal aspects of human emotional experience; the other emphasised the 'constructed' or cultural nature of human emotional expression.

Williamson had explored these philosophical issues on the stage a few years earlier. *Dead White Males* (1995) examined 'political correctness' in a modern university. Rival doctrines of human nature provided a background against which he dramatised the difficulties of contemporary relationships. *Heretic* (1996) examined a fascinating intellectual conflict in which Derek Freeman undermined the premises of Margaret Mead's influential anthropological theories. (Albeit the Sydney press emphasised the more immediate drama of Williamson's conflict with director Wayne Harrison over the latter's 'visually lurid' production.) In both *Dead White Males* and *Heretic*, the playwright could be interpreted as promoting a 'passionate middle ground' in psychological theory. One can readily acknowledge the influence of culture on individuals while insisting equally that many traits are human universals.

Basic emotions or affects

One particular aspect of psychological theory prompted me to contact Williamson. His review article in the *Australian* advocated much the same model of psychology that had informed our practice since the early 1990s. We had observed a common emotional sequence in Conferences and a tendency for what is now called 'affective resonance'. The degree of emotional difference between participants seemed to diminish through the course of the Conference. One theory seemed to explain these phenomena particularly well.

The theory had been outlined by psychologist and philosopher Silvan Tomkins in *Affect, Imagery, Consciousness* (1961–1991), recently described as 'a four-volume work so dense that its readers were evenly divided between those who understood it and thought it was brilliant and those who did not understand it and thought it was brilliant'.[22] In the first two volumes of *Affect, Imagery, Consciousness*, Tomkins argued persuasively that human emotional life is based on a discrete set of evolved physiological programs, called affects.

Some psychologists refer to affects as 'basic emotions', but there is merit in using a separate word. It helps distinguish the physiology of affect from the more complex psychology of emotions. Affects involve universally recognised facial expressions. Each affect is triggered by a particular profile of activity in our nervous system. Whether there is an increase in neural activity, a decrease, or a steady state, an affect amplifies the signal that is causing that activity. Our attention will be directed to the source of the signal.

For instance, too much of any stimulus will generate a 'steady above optimal' signal. Any signal with this particular profile triggers the affect of distress. A baby will whimper with distress, regardless of whether the 'steady above optimal' level of activity in the nervous system is signalled by too much cold, too much heat, too much hunger, thirst, pain, tiredness or neglect. Each of the other affects—anger, fear, surprise, interest and enjoyment—is likewise triggered by a particular profile of activity in our nervous system. Additionally, the theory explains why facial expressions of disgust, 'dissmell', and shame are universally recognised. It explains how all these phenomena are, to some degree 'contagious': they influence other people as well as ourselves.

Even when it was proposed some decades back, Tomkins' theory was very complex in its details, and since then the volume of data in the field of neurology has grown immensely. But the basic idea that the human emotional system is built on a core set of physiological programs is generally supported by the data.

From our perspective, the general principles were more important than the details. We had been searching in the early 1990s for a coherent theory to explain phenomena that were strikingly displayed in a Conference. What theory best explained how emotions can override logic, how habits seem based around standard emotional patterns, and how a small group of people can experience 'emotional contagion', with destructive consequences in some settings, but very constructive consequences in others?

Among the fruits of an extensive literature search was the recently published *Shame and Pride*, by Philadelphia–based psychiatrist Donald Nathanson.[23] This book provided a clear introduction to the work of Tomkins. His work, in turn, proved a hugely helpful guide both to understanding the dynamics of Conferencing, and to managing situations fraught with conflict.

Perhaps not surprisingly, it turned out that Williamson had read the first volumes of *Affect, Imagery, Consciousness* years before, while studying psychology at Melbourne University. He was one of those readers who understood it and thought it was brilliant.[24] And some of the reasons for his interest were very personal. As he confesses, the legacy of the family dynamics portrayed in *After the Ball* left 'a tendency to avoid conflict in real life, [but to remain] obsessed [by] the causes of conflict and its consequences'.[25]

Simplifying Complexity: Face to Face

Like other powerful theories, the theory of the affect system distilled simple principles from highly complex material. When used to analyse the dynamics of a Conference, the theory brought clarity to the complex emotional dynamics of a group. To a playwright personally 'obsessed by the causes and consequences of conflict', this was pure gold. And so, Williamson broke his pattern of writing plays that dealt, alternately, with an institution then with an individual. *Face to Face* grapples, instead, with philosophy and process, with a grand theory of motivation that explains a very particular group dynamic.

Director Sandra Bates applied this same principle of simplifying complexity to the premiere production of *Face to Face*. Against a plain black backdrop, the standard circle of chairs was split open. Participants were seated in a half-circle, with the audience completing the circle. Williamson incorporated this radically simple style in his stage directions for the subsequent two plays of the trilogy.

There are several key sources of raw material for *Face to Face*:

◆ case studies of Conferences convened by TJA and dealing with workplace conflict;
◆ edited transcripts of youth justice Conferences from a 1995 report to the Criminology Research Council;[26]

◆ Williamson's observations of real and role-played Conferences
convened by TJA; and
◆ the setting of a scaffolding firm inspired by stories from Williamson's
son Rory.

Typically, plenty of additional creativity was needed to generate the
detail in some of the scenes.

The TJA Conference case studies from workplaces were collected
through 1995 and 1996 and I presented them in an address to the
Tomkins Institute in Philadelphia.[27] The paper makes interesting
reading now. It shows us still analysing workplace conflict with the
terminology of undisputed harm cases. We were searching for the clearest
cases of harm in each situation, but we were already sensing that this
stretched the terminology and oversimplified complex situations. So
we began to change the language of analysis: 'the offender' became the
more generalized 'person who acted first' and the 'victim(s)' became
'the person or people most directly affected'.

Intriguingly, *Face to Face* captures this transition in our own thinking.
The language of the play is half in and half out of the criminal legal
system. Indeed, the drama is most intense when Jack reminds
participants of the stakes: if we don't resolve this as a workplace matter,
it becomes a criminal matter, with terrible consequences for Glen.

What was the optimal structure to dramatise these complexities?
Should a play about Conferencing include the drama of preparation,
the intense moments in individual interviews, the frequent need for
last minute brinkmanship before a Conference, and all the other
difficulties faced by the Convenor?

Williamson explains his aesthetic choices by comparing the different
logics of stage and film. Simplicity, he felt, would be the key to a
successful stage portrayal of Conferencing. Reflecting back on *Face to
Face* while writing *A Conversation* he wrote:

> In film or television the flashbacks and viewpoint reruns can be
> effectively managed, but I've got a gut feeling that the format I used in
> *Face to Face* is going to work best on stage and it's certainly the feedback
> I'm getting from the directors who have read it. I think that there's a
> certain magic in just presenting the Conference itself on stage. The
> actors can't get on or off and the audience has to piece together the
> story from the actual Conference events. I remember how interesting
> it was for me at the school Conference to see the events unfold there
> and then. Because the stage has no close ups and can't direct the

audience's attention in the forceful way that film can, it can tell the story of all the characters on stage more or less equally.[28]

In short, film and television can better capture the emotional subtleties of individuals, but a stage production can better capture a collective dynamic. Members of the cast and crew in each premiere production of the trilogy plays were struck by the way the plays 'tell the story of all the characters on stage more or less equally'. In stage productions of the plays, there is no central character.

> Film and television seem to work better as narratives seen from a central character's viewpoint. [This is] because so much can be told just from the central character's facial expressions in close up. I envisage the TV version being told from the viewpoint of a convener. In this case, the audience will be privy to his/her frustrations as experienced during the research phase and the post-Conference phase. We will know which of the participants the convener expects to have most trouble with, and will be on edge seeing if the prediction is right. In other words, I think that on stage it might be best seen as the story of the process itself whereas on the screen it becomes the convener's story.[29]

To tell the story of the process itself, Williamson examined edited transcripts of audio-recorded Conferences, and then observed 'live' Conferences, both 'real' and 'role-played' (the latter being a simulated Conference used to train Convenors).

The transcripts of Conferences were derived from audio recordings made during the evaluation of the Wagga Conferencing program, and were included in the report on that program.[30] While transcribing these recordings some years earlier, I had become particularly sensitised to the language used by participants. The transcripts hinted that Conference participants move through a standard emotional sequence. Interviews with Conference participants reflecting on their experiences tended to support this theory of a profound similarity beneath the superficial differences from one case to another.

Williamson observed Conferences convened under the aegis of two separate programs in New South Wales. Through 1998 and 1999, the Student Services Division of the Department of Education and Training supported an evaluated program of Conferencing to deal with incidents for which suspension or exclusion might be considered and Williamson observed a Conference convened as part of this program. (The program quickly and markedly reduced the number of student days lost through suspension and exclusion in participating schools.)

Williamson also observed preparation for the larger Youth Justice Conferencing program run by the Department of Juvenile Justice. In a training workshop for the program's District Administrators, Williamson participated in a full-length, full-size role-play of a Conference dealing with a fairly typical case of property damage.

In short, the playwright immersed himself thoroughly in the theory and practice of the Conferencing process. He became familiar with the stories of many specific cases that had been brought to a Conference. All this was new. And yet, *The Jack Manning Trilogy* plays echo themes already visited in his earlier plays.

For instance, the play *Brilliant Lies* (1993), which was filmed in 1996, portrays 'a dysfunctional family that discovers there are still some ties that continue to bind'.[31] In one scene, an official of the Anti-Discrimination Board attempts to mediate a charge of sexual harassment. The scene vividly captures the mediator's awkwardness, as she tries to use a process that is not appropriate for the presenting case.

Corporate Vibes (1999) likewise presages themes from *Face to Face* and *Charitable Intent*. The characters of *Corporate Vibes* are the architectural staff and owner of a Sydney construction firm that specialises in building large residential apartment blocks. The central conflict in the play is between owner Sam Siddons' autocratic style, and the 'modern management' ethos passionately espoused by his new Human Resources manager. Her attempts to foster this new ethos are portrayed with satire so gentle that it almost ceases to be satire. The play seems to pose a good-humored question: is there really something behind all this talk of 'emotional intelligence at work'? The staff at Siddons themselves seem caught in a middle ground 'between satire and sympathy'. As more than one critic noted, the other 'workplace' play of 1999, *Face to Face*, firmly occupies this aesthetic position between satire and sympathy.

Two Conversations

In Robyn Nevin's memorable production of *Corporate Vibes* at the Sydney Opera House, the scene changes and sets were mechanistic and stylised, a metaphor both for the construction process, and for the disciplines of corporate life. This aspect of the production highlighted a recurrent style and themes that were already evident in Williamson's early plays:

> The reader, rather than look for momentous lines, is encouraged to feel for a groundswell of emotion underlying the dialogue, and to view the

dialogue as often being no more than a ritualistic form of defence against peaks of emotion that threaten to blast the protagonists out of their stereotyped roles. For this reason, the tone and rhythms of the dialogue are often more important than its content.[32]

A Conversation can be understood as the culmination of this tendency. In many ways, *A Conversation* is the play least like anything Williamson had previously written. No other play seems as bleakly intense, nor as strangely uplifting. In many other Williamson plays emotion threatens to blast protagonists out of stereotyped roles. The difference here is that the threat is realised. The protagonists are blasted out of their roles and transformed by a shared understanding.

A Conversation was inspired more by a series of key ideas than by any detailed source material case study. For many years, in disparate local programs in North America, groups using 'Victim Offender Mediation' had brought together the perpetrators and victim of crimes.[33] We told Williamson about this work which involved serious crimes for which the perpetrators had been jailed. Then in 1999, an Australian documentary publicised to a national audience the idea of Conferencing for serious crimes.

Facing the Demons showed a Conference involving people affected by the murder of Michael Marslew, a young man shot at close range during an armed robbery of a Sydney Pizza Hut. Ken Marslew, Michael's father, subsequently founded the crime prevention organisation *Enough is Enough*. A Sydney police Sergeant suggested to Ken the possibility of participating in a Conference. As Head of the Community Policing program in Wagga in the early 1990s, Terry O'Connell had been the police officer most involved in the Conferencing pilot there. He convened the Conference in *Facing the Demons*, which was filmed by Aviva Ziegler.

The documentary gave further impetus to an idea that was already under consideration in the Department of Corrective Services. Shortly after *Face to Face* had played at the Ensemble, a senior Corrective Services official suggested that her Department might host a Conferencing program. To further familiarise herself with the process, Rhonda Booby attended a TJA Conference Conveners' Training Workshop. She then arranged for a group of her colleagues, most of them clinical psychologists, to be trained as Convenors.

Rhonda then formed a Restorative Justice Unit within the Department. The Unit publicised the availability of Conferencing both through the prison system and through victim support groups. John McDonald convened the first Conference under the auspices of this program. It involved a tragic case of culpable driving causing death. Discussions about the dilemmas and difficulties of this case seem to have been a significant prompt for *A Conversation*.

From early in the creative process, Williamson seems to have envisaged two versions of *A Conversation*. As so often in his work, he managed to juxtapose several previously unrelated issues and then place them in a new context. The continuing use of the death penalty in the United States was one impetus to set a separate version of the play there. Last used in Australia in the 1960s, the death penalty remains a significant and controversial reality in the United States, and it adds another moral dimension to *A Conversation*. If an appeal for clemency can determine whether a person convicted of murder lives or dies, this places a great burden on those who might appeal for clemency.

Other general 'law and order' issues at the time of writing prompted Williamson to set a version of *A Conversation* in the United States, and specifically California. These issues, some of them subject to public ballot, included mandatory sentencing guidelines, gun control and the public identification of released offenders. In each case, there were significant differences between the Australian and American experiences.

More specifically, we had been intrigued by the nature of some inter-group conflict in the north-eastern United States. We had discussed with Williamson our experiences of helping to establish Conferencing programs in Maryland and Pennsylvania. We had frequently observed that in Conferences addressing undisputed harm, differences between groups would initially increase the conflict between participants. But at some point, participants would see deeper similarities beneath superficial differences of class, culture and particularly of ethnicity. And once participants saw these similarities, the differences between groups would no longer fuel the conflict.

This observation raised an obvious question: when two families are affected by a truly terrible crime, and seek to deal with it together, can they begin to overcome their class, cultural or ethnic differences? Or will the differences overcome them? Williamson sought to answer this question in both versions of *A Conversation*.

In the Australian version, the key difference between the two families is class: Derek and Barbara reside in a wealthier part of Sydney; the

Williams family lives out West. In the US version of the play, the families are divided not only by class differences, but by ethnic differences as well. One family is wealthy; one struggles financially. One is Jewish; one is African American. It is the ethnic difference that initially seems most important to the protagonists. Would ethnicity seem the most important difference to an audience? And would a play portraying this ethnic difference be seen as provocative, creating its own political drama?

Several powerful performed readings of *A Conversation* in the States prompted extensive discussions on these topics. In one case, a director colleague of Williamson's decided the play was simply too hot to handle, and abandoned a planned reading. This highlighted the artistic and political obstacles to presenting the play in the United States, where ethnic differences tend to move from being an issue to being *the* issue.

We reflected on differing degrees of what might be called 'ethnic essentialism' in the 'new world settler societies'. In Australia, with the exception of some Pacific Island cane farmers in Queensland, one can't tell by appearance alone whether or not a person's ancestors arrived on these shores in chains. Conversely, in the United States, most citizens of African ethnicity had ancestors who were enslaved.

This visible legacy has made for very different social histories. In Australia, the *big* ethnic issue relates to dispossession from the land. In Canada there is likewise a big ethnic issue of dispossession and, since the 1830s, there has also been the issue of Quebec, which has given a European ethnic twist to the political divide between Republicans and Monarchists.

In the United States, in contrast, the legacy of slavery consistently eclipses the issue of land dispossession. And class has been compounded with ethnicity so profoundly that class itself is overshadowed. The core challenge in the US version was to address these issues of identity dramatically, without characters and audience members taking up the usual positions in the trenches based on their (existential) ethnic identities rather than their (possibly temporary) class identities.

Williamson expressed this succinctly: 'The race question is only a red herring that the parties have to work through *before* they can start to relate as common human beings'. But even if the *characters* (and the actors who played them) moved past this red herring, the *audience* might not. We were concerned about those who would swallow the red herring whole.

We were greatly heartened by two readings of the play in November

2000, one with the New York Theater Workshop in Manhattan, the other with the Axis Theater in Baltimore. These public readings were profoundly moving performances in their own right, and there was passionate audience discussion after each. The readings were not only different in *degree* from a private solo reading of the play. They were startlingly different in *kind*. The *audience*, like the players, did seem to confront and work through the red herring of ethnic difference.

The general consensus from those who saw the readings was that the play urgently needed to be staged in the US. The play was clearly not about naming-blaming-shaming around the general issue of racism. Rather, when the Convenor asked detailed questions about a personal tragedy specific to two families, their common humanity shone through.

We continued to discuss these issues with friends, especially in Philadelphia and Baltimore. A colleague whose ancestry is a not uncommon mix of European, African and Native American asked if the ethnic roles could be reversed. What if the victims were black, the perpetrator and his family white?

But to buy into this argument might be to accept that the play is primarily about ethnicity. It suggests that the playwright can promote public education with a play not of stereotypes, but of reverse stereotypes. Instead, the play issues a broader challenge to received wisdom. It suggests that 'racism' might sometimes best be addressed not head-on, but with a side step, such that people can re-categorise themselves and each other. They can begin to identify as siblings, parents, and people with shared experiences. We had seen precisely this shift occur in countless Conferences over the years. The general lesson may have profound consequences for how we deal with difference.

We remained intrigued that although the play, when performed, answers such concerns, many of those who simply *read* the text of the play did not always *hear* those answers. At one level, the reason seems clear. People are ultimately motivated by feelings, not thoughts and when the two aren't in harmony, feelings hold sway. The experience of reading *A Conversation* seemed to evoke a different mix of emotions than the experience of seeing a live performance.

So what was it about the play *on the page* that some people deemed it beyond the pale? On further reflection, the combination of two powerful themes seemed to take on a special significance in the United States. First, 'structural conflict' between groups exacerbates the conflict caused by a deadly act. Second, this 'structural conflict' is combined with the tragic case of a clinical psychologist who has made the wrong judgement call and is damned for the consequences.

In the US version of *A Conversation*, this juxtaposition seems to strike a particular chord. Some readers of the play perceived the combination of ethnic conflict and psychological pathology to reproduce a cultural stereotype of the 'crazed' black man. As we listened to their concerns, it became increasingly clear that they were struggling to articulate the following request. *Either* make the perpetrator a psychopath, *or*, alternatively, show that his behaviour is ultimately historically explicable, the tragic result of psycho-socio-politico-economical circumstances. Make the problem the result of nature or nurture. But not both!

One of Williamson's responses to these concerns was to make the 'red herring' of ethnic difference a little less diverting. Subsequent drafts of the American version of the play minimised character features that some people might perceive as offensively stereotypical. Another response was to urge any colleagues who were considering producing the play to proceed with a reading performance. Some actors involved in the New York and/or Baltimore performances had preliminary concerns, but found them swept away by the power of the play.

Much of what was expunged from the earlier American version was also expunged from the Australian version but reinstated during rehearsals for the 2001 premiere production in Sydney. The various drafts of the play itself went through a transformation that, strangely, parallels the experience of the Conference participants. Conflict between different ethnic groups came to the fore. For a time it became the key issue. Then the issue faded, and common humanity reasserted itself.

There is a powerfully ironic postscript to this saga about *A Conversation*, and Williamson's extensive rewriting to strike the right balance in the sensitive issue of conflict between groups. The premiere season of *A Conversation* began in Sydney less than a week after 11 September 2001.

Origins of Charitable Intent

In contrast to the convoluted genesis and evolution of *A Conversation*, Williamson produced his working draft of *Charitable Intent* with remarkable speed. Indeed, the circumstances called for speed. Organisers of the 2001 Melbourne Festival wanted a new Williamson play to mark the thirtieth anniversary of Williamson's first performance at La Mama. *Face to Face* had already been staged in Melbourne in a successful Playbox production directed by Aubrey Mellor and much publicised because Guy Pearce played the role of Jack.

If another Conferencing play in Melbourne might seem too much of a good thing, the format seemed ideally suited to the intimate setting of La Mama, the upstairs room in inner-city Carlton that has been the venue for much new local theatre since the 1960s. So what could differentiate a third Conferencing play sufficiently from the other two?

A key creative decision concerned the setting. *Face to Face* is set in a blue-collar workplace. *A Conversation*, dealing with a shocking criminal justice case, involves people from disparate social backgrounds. Several of them describe scenes from work, and most of these scenes are from small businesses or the service sector. In contrast, Williamson chose to set *Charitable Intent* in a white-collar workplace. More interestingly, this particular white-collar workplace is neither a corporate 'for-profit', organisation, nor a government sector organisation. Rather, Enabling and Caring is a 'third sector' organisation, part of the 'not-for-profit' community sector.

The question of an appropriate business and management model for community sector organisations is the subject of ongoing debate. There is an intrinsic 'structural' tension between the guardian ethos of government sector agencies and the commercial ethos of profit-making organisations.[34] They work with different currencies. Government agencies deal in political capital; commercial organisations deal in financial capital. Community sector organisations sit somewhere in between—or off to one side.

Community organisations provide important social services in areas where there is some sort of 'market failure', but to provide those services successfully, they need a spirit of entrepreneurialism. Government agencies are granted a monopoly in their area of service provision. Community sector organisations tend to compete against each other for government contracts and charitable donations.

While any cultural clash can make for interesting drama, the particular tension between corporate and community sector cultures happened to be topical when *Charitable Intent* was penned. An experienced businesswoman had recently been appointed to head the major Australian charity, the Smith Family. But Williamson added an additional layer of drama to the clash between two cultures. While the drama of *Charitable Intent* certainly derives in part from the cultural or *political* clash between participants who personify aspects of corporate and community sector culture, it derives at least as much from the *psychology* of those individuals.

The play answers a psychological question about Conferencing that Brian, the Chairman of the Enabling and Caring Board, poses at the outset. What if there really is some deep-seated problem that can't be resolved by a simple agreement? As Williamson wrote while drafting *Charitable Intent*: 'I'd like a play that says "hey, this is one of the [cases] where a thoroughgoing character disorder makes [a happy outcome] unlikely". But even in this situation, surely Conferences are valuable to make it plain to all that there is a psychological disturbance at the core'.[35] In a situation like this, Conferencing functions as a sifting or winnowing mechanism. Ultimately, the process performs an administrative function, separating socio-political problems from psychological problems.

Case notes from some particularly difficult Conferences had prompted this focus on how problematic psychology can poison workplace politics. Williamson was intrigued to hear of a character who was 'quick to give an insincere smile ... rules by seduction ... is extremely manipulative ... [and] never says anything constructive about anyone except herself'.[36] Our experience suggested that certain organisational structures encourage characters like Bryony to self-select. A person wishing to wield power *over* others may be drawn to an organisation that grants such power. The same organisational structures can then exacerbate problematic elements of an individual's style.

In such situations, if people really can't work together, our instincts and practice have been not to keep them together. Conferences have helped to distinguish socio-political problems from psychological ones. On this occasion, it turns out that the problem is indeed significantly psychological. Towards the end of the Conference, the psychological dimension becomes half clear even to Bryony. But the political problem is stark. Once Bryony realises she's burnt all her bridges, she seems set to jump rather than be pushed.

Bryony's gradual unmasking is inherently dramatic. Her political downfall seems increasingly inevitable, but it is compelling to watch. And even in the first draft of *Charitable Intent*, the drama seemed to unfold at just the right pace. The structure of the play was sound.

Our one extensive conversation over the first draft concerned Jack's statements on the subject of bullying. Jack says more in *Charitable Intent* about the process of Conferencing than he does in the other two plays. He offers a more extensive summary of the situation in which participants find themselves. He also comments more fully on the apparent outcome of the Conference. And the concern here was that Jack might seem too accepting of the 'Bryony is malicious' thesis, with the implication that, when she goes, the problems at Enabling and Caring should go with her. Would audiences infer that this was a typical 'bullying' case, with a typical solution?

'Bryony is malicious' is the second of two basic theses to which the audience might be drawn. It's the antithesis to a plausible initial hypothesis: 'Well, Amanda is rather lazy'. The common thread here is an implication that bullying behaviour is essentially a psychological phenomenon. Either 'offenders' are compelled to make life miserable for others, or 'victims' bring the bullying behaviour on themselves.

But much of what gets labelled 'bullying' is more complicated. So should the playwright seek to be didactic about the language of bullying? Should Jack suggest that the Enabling and Caring case is not necessarily typical, that it represents only one of several ways that 'bullying' occurs?

Certainly, the term 'bullying' applies to situations where the fundamental conflict is *within* a person like Bryony. But the word also describes situations where conflict has evolved *between* people through a set of unfortunate circumstances. In such situations, conflict can seem inevitable, given vast differences in personal style, and individual allegiances to groups in conflict. In short, the word 'bullying' is used for several distinct phenomena. Ironically, such linguistic confusion tends, in and of itself, to cause conflict.

So it is certainly dramatically effective that Bryony turns out to be bad, much as it is dramatically effective that Scott is genuinely bad in *A Conversation*. But in *A Conversation* it is clear that a Conference could be equally valuable with perpetrators who are not sociopathic. In *Charitable Intent*, on the other hand, Jack doesn't strongly challenge the implication that, bullying is essentially a psychological problem, and the solution is to remove the bully.

In a workplace where there have been accusations of bullying, individuals have three choices of action. The first two choices involve *destructive* engagement: side with the accuser, or side with the accused against a common enemy. In the *Charitable Intent* Conference, all the participants from Enabling and Caring have engaged destructively, feeling compelled to side with either Bryony or Amanda. And the play powerfully demonstrates that Conferencing can indeed flush out someone who doesn't really want constructive engagement.

Bryony proves to be fundamentally contemptuous of whole groups of people with whom she's dealing: young women with ambition; middle-aged women without ambition; men—indeed, pretty much anyone. But much Bryony-like behaviour we've come across is more transparently defensive. Of course, to those on the receiving end, the behaviour feels unbearably aggressive. Nevertheless, the individual accused of bullying may genuinely not grasp how they are perceived.

It is also more common, in our experience, for individuals in a conflicted workplace to be diplomatic. Rather than side with either of the chief antagonists, they choose to *dis*engage. This, too, can be damaging. Over time, many *individual* choices to disengage produce the *collective* result of a workplace where people no longer talk to one another. These situations are generally identified as 'decreasing morale', but might more accurately be called 'increasing conflict'. This conflict is less obvious only because it manifests primarily as disengagement, rather than destructive engagement. Yet much legal and administrative policy seems to focus exclusively on individual choices. 'Who's done the wrong thing and what should we do to them?' may be the wrong questions to ask if there's a systemic problem, but it is a common response.

In our experience, the role of Boards is equally complex. Like individuals in positions of authority, Boards may appear to engage in bullying behaviour and to be contemptuous of people, often because Boards act as a collective and impose decisions on people. To the people on the receiving end, a Board's decisions may feel like bullying. Yet Board members may not have intended their decisions to have that effect. They may be oblivious to any perception that they are 'bullying'.

Jack's comments toward the end of the play suggest he has seen many cases of alleged bullying. So he might well suggest that these situations can be more complicated than they seem. Yes, some Boards may include bullying personalities. Other Boards may encourage their members to behave in a bullying way under peer pressure. The classic studies in social psychology show how readily people can adopt different roles in different settings. (Indeed, the young trio of Tamsyn, Cassie and Giulia seem to demonstrate exactly this phenomenon in the Enabling and Caring workplace.) Jack might hesitate to accept an explanation of bullying that denied this complexity.

As in *Face to Face*, then, a key decision was how to resolve the tension between didacticism and drama. Jack is faced with temptation in *Charitable Intent*. He can't help but be unimpressed with Bryony's behaviour, and Brian's unwillingness to see the damage she has caused. Should Jack remain steadfastly neutral? Should he resist the temptation to take sides against a participant? Should he challenge the simplistic view that bullying is essentially a problem of psychology? Generally, when presented with a tension between explaining and entertaining, the playwright's intuition is to favour entertainment. And that intuition is usually correct. Williamson allows Jack to succumb to temptation.

As Bryony leaves the Conference, Jack shows some partisanship. He combines sympathy for Amanda and visible annoyance with the way company boards can encourage and exacerbate destructive workplace cultures. His advice to Stella may sound a bit cynical. Or maybe it's just politically astute: 'Have a few lunches with your contact and the chances [of the Board rebelling against another bad choice] might improve' (p.151).

To have Jack drop his guard at the end of this Conference—the closing moments of the trilogy—works dramatically. And *Charitable Intent* seems to have had a cathartic effect for audiences. As John McCallum, theatre critic for the *Australian* newspaper, put it, the play ends with 'a revelation of incompetent management and the moral vindication of the old ways'. But the moral vindication may be less for the 'old ways' than of someone who stubbornly stands up for herself.

Amanda is subjected to political intrigue, humiliation, and betrayal. She stands her ground, and she retains her dignity. Cheering audiences suggested that Amanda's experience at Enabling and Caring is not uncommon. When she admits feeling 'as if I've just come out of a long dark tunnel' (p.152), audiences applaud her dignified victory.

4. Interviews

The following interviews were conducted between March and May 2002, by e-mail, phone and face to face.

David Williamson

When we first talked with you about Conferencing, what elements of the process most fired your imagination?

The fact that the process acknowledged the primacy of emotions in human behaviour. So much of psychology and the social sciences go about their business pretending the emotions don't exist. That we're all 'socially constructed' by information that lodges in our cortex as if we are totally cognitive creatures. Here was a process that depends on its recognition of the power of emotions in directing our thoughts and ordering our lives. And a process that works to transform conflict by allowing the emotions to progress from very negative to positive in an ordered sequence. And the fact that you and John had gone back to one of my favourite thinkers on the emotions, Silvan S. Tomkins, and worked out just why the process was so effective. I was impressed by the amount of high level thinking that had gone on to explain, hone and perfect the process. I was also excited by it as a dramatist. So much of our social life consists of attempts to disguise and submerge our emotions, and a process that allowed the primal power of emotions to emerge at full strength is a very powerful dramatic arena. I felt that if I got it right, I could not only create strong drama but also make a dramatic statement that suggested that there was a much better way to deal with conflict available and ready to go.

Why a trilogy?

I'm not quite sure why I thought of a trilogy almost immediately. I think it was something to do with the fact that you guys made it clear to me very early on that this process works in many arenas. It can deal with criminal acts of undisputed harm, and it can deal with workplace situations where there is no obvious act of undisputed harm, but a continuing and debilitating atmosphere of conflict. It can also deal with situations that need healing and closure such as that depicted in *A Conversation*, in which the parents of a victim of crime meet the parents of the perpetrator. If I was going to write on the subject I wanted to try and acknowledge these different possibilities in different arenas.

What inspired you to use the 'radical naturalist' format?

One of my early plays, *Don's Party*, uses an ongoing social event and I felt it's something that the stage handles well. I did it again in *The Club* and *The Department*. The conferencing situation is perfect for this type of radical naturalism. You start a social event and let it run on in real time. Unlike traditional narrative, which focuses on the progression of a protagonist, and all the other characters are to some extent bit players, this type of naturalism makes all characters equally important, something which is part of the very basis of Conferencing. Conferencing attempts to give the views and feelings of every participant equal importance.

You've continued to write (another) play each year even as you created this trilogy. Has your other work been influenced by the trilogy and by Conferencing?

Yes I think my other work has been influenced by the Conferencing plays. Conferencing has shown me that there is a strong human need for healing and community; that we would much rather like than hate each other. That hate often arises from a misperception that the other person's motives towards us are more negative than they actually are. Conferencing has made me think more optimistically about human nature and this, I think, has been reflected in the social comedies, which offer a little more redemption to their characters than I might have earlier in life. Of course I still think there are genuinely malignant people out there. All is not just a matter of misperception and sometimes a Conference will uncover malignancy that's not easily fixed as in *Charitable Intent*. But even there the process works to clarify just what is going on.

What technical challenges are presented by writing for a group of actors who are continually on stage with no scene changes?

The group must achieve a seamless ensemble type playing with the group dynamic being the focus all the time rather than star cameos. As there is not a great deal of stage movement, emotional movement must replace physical movement as powerful emotions ebb and flow and keep the audience transfixed.

You chose to set *Face to Face*, the first play in the trilogy, in a blue collar workplace. What inspired that choice?

I read a lot of material about Conferences that had actually happened and listened to you and John talk about Conferences you'd facilitated. Something that grabbed me was the nihilistic sense of desperation present in many workplaces in which the workers felt that they'd failed in life and that there was no way out of the debilitating and menial drudgery. This gave rise to quite vicious interpersonal behaviour in which the weaker workers were mercilessly picked on and humiliated to give the humiliators an outlet for their internal anger and frustration and a sense that at least they were on top in the particular arena in which they were trapped. This led me to feel a strong sense of compassion for some of the most victimised and a sense of hope that Conferencing seemed able to improve morale dramatically even in quite vicious work situations. It felt like an arena ripe for dramatic exploration.

With the second play, you did something quite unusual, and wrote two versions—one for the US and one for Australia. Why that decision? And what did you learn from that experience?

When I was writing the play I realised that the jeopardy for the murderer rapist in the States was much higher, i.e. the death penalty. This raises the stakes. And the thought that the play might work in the US appealed to me as a writer who likes the work to travel and also as someone who believed in this process and thought it might help spread the word about a humane and effective new way of dealing with conflict.

How did it feel returning to La Mama after thirty years with the third play in the trilogy, *Charitable Intent*?

Going back to La Mama was hugely satisfying. It's the theatre that gave me a start and along with those fine Melbourne actors who first did my work—Bruce Spence, Peter Cummins, Fay Byrne, and Paul Hampton— I owed a huge debt to Betty Burstall, La Mama's founder and patron saint. I felt I was returning home to try and thank Betty and the present director, Liz Jones, for all that they'd done for me. It was the perfect space for a Conferencing play. Intimate and intense. And the play worked very well indeed. Terrific cast and Tom Gutteridge did a fine job as director.

Sandra Bates

Sandra Bates directed the premiere productions of Face to Face *and* A Conversation, *both at the Ensemble Theatre in Kirribilli, Sydney.*

When David Williamson showed you the script of *Face to Face*, what were your first impressions?

Well, David never writes how many characters there are at the beginning of a play. We're a totally unsubsidised theatre, and we average about five [actors] per play. My first reaction—which sadly has to be financial—was, as I read over about three pages, 'It's looking to me like there might be *ten* in this cast!' And then I thought, 'It almost doesn't matter, because I'll be able to double up roles'. And then I cottoned on: all *ten* of them are on the stage *all* the time! That was a horrible shock, because there's no way we could make that work financially.

So how do you say to a playwright of Williamson's calibre, who is such a *fabulous* playwright, 'Well, thanks very much for your play but we can't do it'? And then I forgot all that, and started to read it. Once I got into it, I just couldn't believe how drawn in I became to it all. It seems to be set up with goodies and baddies, and then suddenly you begin to see that they're all *people*. And there was also a bit of thinking that some characters were witnesses, as it were, to this. They'd been brought in as witnesses and yet the process made *everybody* look at their own behaviour. Everybody had an opportunity to change. That's pretty exciting when you're used to reading a lot of plays where you've made decisions about goodies and baddies.

Having decided to stage *Face to Face*, how did the experience of directing what Williamson calls a 'radical naturalist' play differ from the other Williamson productions that you've done?

Whether I like it or not, in my job I've got to wear the financial hat along with the artistic hat. I thought, 'Well, is there *any* way at *all* that we could make this work so it that it doesn't kill us financially?' So I thought, 'Actually if we didn't have a designer, or a costume designer, or a lighting designer, or a sound designer, and if we didn't *have* a set, or costumes, or props, or a stage manager, we could *just* break even with ten in the cast!' So the horrendous financial hat took over, and once that had said to me, 'Well, actually we *could* make it work financially if we had none of those things', then immediately the artistic thing said, 'That's the way I *choose* to do it! I actually *want* to do it that way. I would be *appalled* if we did it any other way!'

We used the chairs from the restaurant because that meant we didn't have to buy chairs. We used a table that was out in the back room. It cost us $300. Normally it would be maybe $40 000 for those costs, and ours were $300 for *Face to Face*—for painting the back wall! So the more I looked at that, the more I thought, 'I actually like that!' The more I looked into it, the more I wanted the audience to think that this could be *real*, so that they've eaten their dinner on these restaurant chairs, and that they walk into the theatre and they recognise those same chairs. There's a belief that this could be a real Conference happening. To help all this, I decided to give out the programs at the end of the night and just have a bit of paper to give people beforehand saying that the Conference was being held at the Ensemble Theatre and giving the names of the participants, without any actors' names.

I even overheard a lady one evening saying 'I thought we were coming to a play tonight?' The woman next to her said, 'I think we are'. And she said, 'I don't think so; this is some kind of Conference. Look at this bit of paper! I think we're coming to a Conference of some sort. Why would we do that? We've paid good money to see a play and we're going to see a flipping Conference!!'

I was very interested in their reaction. By half way through, I could hear them beginning to cry. So hey, it was great! You are influenced in a small theatre like this. I was excited when the second play arrived to see that it only had eight in the cast, so we might have even been able to afford a little bit more! But Williamson had written it with all the stage directions exactly as we had done it with *Face to Face*. Because he'd seen that that's a way it will work.

In both those plays, then, you combined this minimal stage design with the radical naturalist format. That combination clearly *did* make the whole experience more intimate for people. How did you prepare the actors for that experience?
I think that any actor who was coming into something like this, as that character, their fear, no matter how minor their role in it, or how minor they thought their role was going to be in it, they would believe that they would probably suffer. And I defy anyone going into a Conference to not be thinking, 'How's this going to affect me? What are they going to ask me? Am I going to suffer out of this?' And I think there's tension at the beginning for each of those people. So I didn't put them into male and female dressing rooms, which is what we normally do. I put

them into their family groups or whomever they were supposed to be with, and they didn't speak to their 'enemy' from the time they arrived.

The animosity that they come on stage with is extraordinary, and the tension, and the ill-feeling—really *ill*-feeling—is there from the beginning, because we have to get through a lot of exposition. And I think that really did pay off very well. The other thing I believe is that there is no way that actors will have experienced all of these experiences. They just won't have experienced them in their lives. And so in each of the three productions I've done, I've encouraged them enormously... For a start, we've done the thing that you would and John would do at TJA, of interviewing participants.

In Sydney Geoff Cartwright, and in Perth Michael Loney, did a private interview—maybe up to an hour—with each [actor] very early in the rehearsal period. And God bless Geoff and Michael, they went along with it entirely. Because the actors didn't know the play that well at that stage, they often took on the characters' points of view very strongly. And sometimes, when the interviewers were asking the questions, they would say things which, later on in the play, turned out not to be true. On stage these lies would come out, and there were moments where the audience, particularly if they were fairly aware, would say, 'What is this? What's this extra tension that's happened which we don't really understand?' And then we improvised around every single thing that is talked about, we improvised around every one of those moments. So when an actor says *any* line in the play, they've done it, they've *lived* it.

The improvising we did was very interesting, because in both [productions of] *Face to Face*, the young men—Duncan [Young] and Luke [Hewett]—they totally lost control several times. They are big men, and we were battling to keep them under control.

Geoff Cartwright did an unusual amount of preparation for both plays. With *Face to Face*, he watched a very large, dramatic Conference we ran for a major Australian institution in a sexual harassment case. Then, for *Conversation*, among other things, he spent time with the Homicide Victims' Support Group. How did that show?
Well, I thought it was very interesting when two of the people that Williamson had based [*A Conversation*] on—a couple—came to the opening night. It was a long while since they had gone through this, but I was very dubious about talking to that couple on opening night,

knowing how *terribly* hard it must have been for them. So terribly hard. And the wife just looked at me, with tears pouring down her face, and said, 'Sandy, you don't understand how healing this is, how much it matters to us that this process happens so that other people like us...'

I think it was something like fourteen years that their lives had been on hold, particularly the father's. And you have no idea how you would be in that situation, no concept of it. But I think the cast members were extraordinary in their ability... I was determined that the people playing the mother and the father of that girl had a daughter each. I remember talking to Di [Craig] about that: trying to get a photo of the girl and taking a photo of *her* daughter, and the guy playing the father's daughter—you can do amazing things now with computers— and making a combined photo that would have bits of both of them so that it wasn't recognisable but it would help them. And Di just looked at me and said, 'Sandra, you could put a photo of a gorilla out there: it's going to be my daughter every night. It's not going to change that'.

And it's true. I mean, David said to me, 'Oh, I'm a bit worried because Di is so upset so quickly, so early in the piece. Where is the growth?' He understands theatre, he understands how it has to go through a process, but he has the young murderer, on tape, at the beginning of the play, and which she's never heard. And I said to him, 'David, I defy *any* mother to listen to that tape and not be totally devastated'. Which is of course what happened, and then during the play each night Di regained her composure. But I just thought her performance was phenomenal. She was so devastating. And so was Robert [Coleby]. He has this beautiful daughter, and I just knew every night he saw her. Not that I'm saying you have to have that, but it added a kind of punch, and much more guilt onto the other characters because they could *see* what they were going through. It's horrendous—and wearing.

There is no way that the convenor can read [the murderer's statement] without in some way being tainted by association. So that device of the taped confession was based on a real case [...]
And the guy was so good, wasn't he? Because he was so... *ordinary*. I got this young man in, and I gave him a couple of notes and he was just so *ordinary*, and that's what made it so awful. If he'd been really awful... but he was just: 'Well, I just kinda liked the look of her and thought, why

wouldn't I?' If it had been done creepily and nastily it wouldn't have had anything like the same effect. It was just evil—evil with an ordinary face.

You had extensive seasons for both plays. What was the typical journey that the audience went on, firstly, for *Face to Face*?
Well, *Face to Face* was funny. It wasn't as tough. *Conversation* was *so* tough. And when I read *Face to Face*, I thought of some of those things, some of the affairs, I thought, 'This is all slightly contrived!' Can you believe, the audience every night went on that journey! They believed it, they wanted to laugh, they wanted the opportunity to laugh, but they believed it, because the cast was so good. And the same with Perth. They're so believable that the audience go on the journey. It's amazing. So, yeah, I think Williamson's a clever bugger!

And even with *Conversation*, which Garry McDonald did read, because I had suggested it, he said, 'Sandra, let me tell you, if there's a laugh line in it I'll find it'. And I said, 'Well, I don't think you'll find a lot of laughs in it, Garry!' So he read it, and he said, 'Well, actually, I didn't even *smile*!' And yet when we did it there were a *number* of laugh lines, and I think the audience were so glad. Because I had thought that the daughter, going on and on on her soapbox, I thought, 'Come on, David, get off *your* soapbox!' But the audience were so relieved to laugh at her. Bianca [Rowe, as Gail,] was believable, and she was passionate. And you're thinking, 'Oh, come off the grass!' But you were so relieved to be able to have a bit of a laugh. And I think with that huge reconciliation, I thought, 'Well, I don't know that I could ever forgive', but you could see that people need to move on with their lives, and this is an opportunity. I just think that it's fantastic.

The final question that [a journalist from Brazil recently] asked me is, 'Should theatre have a social conscience or should it be entertaining?', and I wrote back in the nicest possible way and said that 'the Ensemble theatre is based on the belief that live theatre can and should be a civilising influence in our society'. I'm so sick of saying it now; I've said it a million times, but I absolutely believe it! But that does not mean to say it should not be entertaining. They're *not* mutually exclusive. You can be entertained by being engaged and by going on a journey. It doesn't have to be a bundle of laughs…

After those readings of *A Conversation* in the States, Williamson had made some changes that seemed to be for the sake of political correctness, and that just wouldn't work here in Australia. And some of what had been dropped, I thought, was really important to the crux of what would happen, and it's Australian. Universal, but Australian and not needing to be so politically correct. There were about nine issues, about nine points. So we found the old play and I spent *all night* putting those bits back in. And then we had a long play. Great—but *long*. So then I said to the actors, 'Well David wants it at 90 minutes, and the audience won't take much more than 90 minutes, so you'll just have to overlap'. A couple of the actors said, 'I can't do that; my lines are important! I'm not going to do that!' I said, 'That's what happens in real life; you overlap!' And still two days later I was getting this, 'I can't get my lines out, Sandra! They're not letting me…' I said, 'You get the lines out, you be heard, or we drop those lines. Now they're your alternatives. You want to be heard, you've got 90 minutes to do it, you overlap, you get your lines in, or forget it!'

And there wasn't a single line you couldn't hear clearly in there.
No, you hear it all. You do. You hear it. And that's what would happen in real life, in these Conferences.

Tom Gutteridge

Tom Gutteridge directed the premiere production of Charitable Intent *at La Mama Theatre in Carlton, Melbourne.*

What were your first thoughts on reading *Charitable Intent*?
I remember being both excited and nervous because the play seemed so clear in its narrative line and so open to the performers' and my interpretation. It felt like both a wonderful opportunity and a great responsibility.

How did the experience of staging this 'radical naturalist' ensemble piece compare with your other directing experiences?
I had a ball directing *Charitable Intent* for several reasons. I had just returned to Melbourne and was able to assemble a cast of extraordinary actors (who also happened mostly to be old friends and collaborators). We were to perform in the blessed space of La Mama. Finally, Williamson had written us a play that was funny, punchy and vital. So it's hard for me to make a dispassionate comparison with my other work.

The ensemble nature of the work suited my collaborative instincts as well as the background and abilities of the cast. I also enjoyed the task of rigorously defining the rhythmic shape of the piece; this seemed particularly important to me in a play that is one continuous 75 minute scene. There was also the privilege of the La Mama scale, which meant that we could work in 'close up' for certain moments.

How did the actors prepare for their parts?

Because I didn't get the script until two weeks before we were due to begin rehearsal—Williamson had a big year in 2001!—most of the actors only had the script for a few days before rehearsals began. This meant that nearly all the character development work happened through the rehearsal process. There are a couple of exercises that were particularly productive. One was to improvise the 'pre-Conference interviews' between Jack (Michael Fry) and the other characters. This worked like the well-known 'hot seat' drama exercise to help the characters flesh out their own back-stories and sub-textual motives. For me though, there was an added bonus in seeing the workplace hierarchies exposed via a neutral third party. We also spent one liberating morning using Laban exercises to blow open the static 'Conference' scenario and discovering a strongly physical underlayer to the action.

Laban is a movement analysis system that defines all action (physical and emotional) in terms of four vectors: *weight* (from light to heavy), *time* (from quick to sustained), and *space* (from direct to indirect). There is also *flow* (from free to bound), which has a more subtle role to play. The combinations of the extremes of the first three vectors give you a vocabulary of eight 'effort actions': punch (quick, heavy, direct), glide (sustained, light, direct) etc.

What performers often find is that their character has a tendency towards a few of the effort actions—you might find that one mostly 'punches' and 'dabs' (quick, light, direct) and another 'wrings' (sustained, heavy, indirect) and 'floats' (sustained, light, indirect) and so on. In that particular morning we were exploring the 'tribal' nature of the relationships between characters: Which of them were allies? When did this change? How did people deal with split loyalties?

I asked the cast to physically enact their allegiances at each moment—close to allies, far from foes—and to find gestures to reflect how they were feeling and acting—peacemakers might try stroking or getting between antagonists who might be physically wrestling. (It was chaos!) Within this process I asked them to notice if they favoured particular Laban 'effort actions' and, if they did, to emphasise them. In this way we worked our way through a large section of the play leading up to Amanda's outburst at Bryony, with a kind of human amoeba surging around the rehearsal room occasionally throwing off 'outcasts' or being split into two by the efforts of Jack. By the end of the morning, the cast were mostly pretty clear about what physical/emotional actions their character preferred.

The energy from this exercise strongly informed the actors even though the finished work remained very still.

What particular technical skills did you feel were required (a) to direct, and (b) to play in *Charitable Intent*?

Charitable Intent, like nearly all Williamson's plays, is based on his acute observation of real people in contemporary society, so when casting the play I was first and foremost looking for actors who could create strong characters. But because of the great narrative drive of the play, I was also looking for two other qualities: comic timing and an understanding of structure. My wonderful cast: Michael Fry, Trudy Hellier, Tammy McCarthy, Margaret Mills, Denis Moore, Carole Patullo, Maria Theodorakis and Vivienne Walshe, are all skilled in comedy but, more unusually, they all have experience in making theatre—either as writers, devisors or directors. This meant that from the beginning we were combining exploration of the psychological and emotional layers of the play, with rigorous discussion about the plays themes, gags and narrative lines, and how best to clarify them. This kind of collaborative rehearsal is what I thrive on, and I reckon that the vitality of the finished product was largely due to the ownership that the whole cast felt for the production.

How did you find audiences responded as the emerging story shed a changing light on the key characters?

One of the great pleasures of sitting in the audience was sensing their changing sympathies for the characters. Williamson's narrative keeps peeling back different versions of events, and we wanted to keep the audience guessing as long as possible about where the truth actually lies. We actually asked Williamson to edit a couple of lines to support this sense of ambiguity, and to keep the balance between the two 'sides'. In some of the best shows, the audience would change sides several times!

There were two changes I remember specifically. [The first is on pages 114–115 of the 2002 Currency Press Edition, where] we added a phrase for Brian to make it clear that the board did have reason to want change at Enabling and Caring. The figures are real and came from our research. [Our additions are in italics.]

STELLA: Our last three years before you came were the biggest income increases ever.

BRYONY: We were barely keeping pace with inflation.

STELLA: Three or four percent above inflation.

BRIAN: The Board wanted better than three or four percent. *Across the sector donations have been increasing 14 to 17%.*

[The second change is on page 123, where] we asked to change a line of Stella's so that she is expressing a *belief* rather than a fact. We wanted the audience to have to decide whether they believed her.

BRIAN: It is a very disappointing attitude you're taking, Stella. Corporate donations are a vital part of our income stream.

STELLA: We were doing just as well in that area before Bryony came here and started the great credit card blow-out.

BRYONY: Corporate sponsorship has gone up markedly.

STELLA: Deduct expenses and *I bet* we're almost exactly where we were.

How does the artifice of rhythm and structure enhance the 'naturalism' of the play?

For me rhythm is actually one of the most important storytelling tools for a director. Emphasising rhythm through changes of tempo or energy helps to accentuate particular moments that the audience—hopefully!—picks up on. In most plays the rhythm of the story is also indicated by scene and act changes. In the absence of these we needed to be even more rigorous and specific than usual. In practice this meant defining 'units of action' where dialogue overlapped or where there were marked tempo changes, using changes of volume, and only allowing pauses if they 'meant' something.

Interestingly, while ultimately it's the story that I'm looking to clarify through rhythm, the process of discovering and agreeing on the moments of change is undoubtedly important as part of the performers' 'naturalistic' process. Because by agreeing to the exact moment where a new energy comes in or a gap appears, the cast are also defining the exact nature and intensity of their emotional turning points. It's the kind of work that all actors do instinctively for themselves, but by making it a collective process and ensuring that there's agreement on the exact moment and type of change (which may be 'renegotiated' through rehearsal), the cast become responsible for the overall reading of the play, as well as for their particular character journeys.

Geoff Cartwright

Geoff Cartwright played Jack Manning in the premiere productions of Face to Face *and* A Conversation, *both at the Ensemble Theatre in Kirribilli, Sydney.*

What do you see as the key differences between *Face to Face* and *A Conversation*, conceptually, dramatically, and structurally?

Dramatically the plays are both similar yet radically different. *Face to Face* articulates the story of an abused young man who has acted abusively, brought in front of the people he's harmed, in order to show remorse, apologise and find a way, if not to make reparation, then at least to offer strategies to effect change. Williamson allows for satire within that—Greg Baldoni and his relationship with Julie the office secretary and his attempts to hide that relationship from his wife. Baldoni acts truthfully—for him, which is to lie—but the situation, the duplicity of the characters and how that duplicity manifests itself is hilarious. There was not one audience that didn't find that section of the play uproarious. There is liberal humour within *Face to Face* and the satirical sections are part of that.

A Conversation, though, is free of satire. It tells the story of the family of a young man who has violently raped and murdered a young woman and the family of the young woman. Those families come together (without the murderer) to seek a 'shared understanding' of the events, to assuage guilt, to express remorse, to be heard, to vent anger. It's a painful journey, yet ultimately a healing one. The characters are real people and their story is one where satire has no place. The emotions are huge, as huge as Greek tragedy. As players we were acutely aware of the fact that we were telling real people's stories and that with that privilege comes immense responsibility. Williamson believes in these people in a way that differs from the *Face to Face* characters where he allows himself some licence to play. Both plays offer the audience a journey that is thoroughly engaging and deeply affecting.

Structurally and conceptually there is little or no difference between the two. They are both based strictly on the TJA Conference model and dramatically the events fit into that model. People enter at roughly the same time, sit in a semi-circle facing the audience, engage for the length of the play during which no one leaves, then exit. They are effectively the same play with differing narratives or contexts. Those differing narratives trigger differing states of emotion within the characters, which in turn offers both actors and audience a different experience. In both plays there is a move towards healing or reparation.

Jack Manning says 'And we'll see if we can repair the harm that's been done', exactly as might be said in an actual Conference. That's the play's purpose and the Conference's purpose—to repair, to seek other possibilities—and each play is structured the same way in an attempt to realise those possibilities.

What do you see as the key difference between these two plays, on the one hand, and other Williamson work?
Williamson believes fervently in this process of Conferencing. He is a proselyte. He's on a mission. His other work allows him to observe from a distance, to be cynical, satirical and in *A Conversation* there is no place for satire. It's too real. Williamson is being a healer with these plays, as well as the very fine storyteller that he always is, and the wit and the master of the one-liner.

Tell us a bit about your experience of researching your role for each play.
For *Face to Face*, the primary focus was to understand what Conferencing meant, to get some notion of the theory behind it and from case studies to understand the practice of it. In addition I needed to understand how a convenor of a Conference, whose task is to remain neutral, uses gesture and what his/her physical demeanour is. You and John from TJA spoke with the whole company and were freely available to refer to. I was in effect playing you, so the source was readily available and I made liberal use of that whenever a question occurred to me.

I was permitted to observe a Conference and note that the one and half hours in the theatre may take five, six hours or more in reality. The process was the same—the relation of what happened by the person who caused the harm, the expression of remorse and the shared agreement as to further action as a result. What also interested me were a few individual things. I was able to travel out of Sydney to the Conference with the convenors, noting the tone of the conversation before the Conference, the sense of nervousness, the going over of the details and the music you chose for the journey, either to mirror your own mood then or to prepare the mood for what was to follow. Later you prepared a seating plan for the Conference, discussing the value of who should sit where. I came to use these things for myself.

At the start of both plays Jack Manning (in the Ensemble productions) spends five or ten minutes on stage before the other characters arrive. It's then I draw the seating plan and make notes. I also played music. In *Face to Face* it was the Larghetto from Chopin's Piano Concerto number 2 in F minor, opus 21 played by Ivo Pogorelich with the Chicago Symphony Orchestra. It's a very layered piece and offered a gentle and exquisite beauty that I found made me calm and clear-sighted. It has passages too, which suggested to me apprehension, tension and the possibility of discord, even chaos that might happen if the Conference were to fail. It was appropriate for me and with the sense of ownership each of us was given by Sandra Bates I was the only one it needed to be appropriate for. For *A Conversation* I used Yo-Yo Ma's performance of the second of Bach's Cello suites.

I also noted the music chosen for the car journey home after the successful Conference—the exhilaration of success, the sense of being moved by the journeys of the Conference participants, the expressions of frustration at the participants who could be so close to a healing but kicked against it. Music of celebration and passion and bravery.[38]

These feelings didn't seem foreign to me, the actor, after an opening night. A good opening night. And a convenor needs the concentration of a wicket keeper, constantly on the lookout for which way something will turn. What does that whisper mean, or that grunt or those rolled eyes? What's going on beneath the words? It's an exhausting task in reality despite the appearance of doing very little.

The preparation for *A Conversation* was different in that I was familiar with what a convenor's task was. I needed this time to understand the stories of the participants. Martha Jabour at the Homicide Victims' Support Group spoke with me at length of the people who came to them and invited me to one of their monthly meetings. I was acutely concerned that I might be intruding but these families seemed very happy to speak to me about their situations and graciously did so after the meeting. It was a very distressing meeting for the participants who told their stories in turn. I felt a foreigner as I had no pain in my life that could be understood in the same context as the horror of the stories I heard.

The whole company read the stories of some horrific murders in recent Australian history—the stories of Anita Cobby, Janine Balding, Ebony Simpson and others, trying to get some insight into how such pain for a grieving family would manifest itself; trying to listen to the horror, to picture it, knowing it was real; to inform our choices. Over a period of about a week during this time of preparation I'd find myself crying unexpectedly at odd times. I haven't spoken to the other actors about what responses they were having but I can't imagine mine were unique. It mirrored the journey the audiences would take. The Restorative Justice Unit of the Department of Corrective Services were also very generous in speaking to me, answering questions, pointing me in directions and providing me with resources to continue research.

There was much less for Jack Manning to do in *A Conversation*. The participants' emotions were so close to the surface, so ready to be articulated that little more than 'Let's start' was needed for the Conference to play itself. In *Face to Face* the participants needed to be encouraged, cajoled, even bullied to speak. It's much more hands-on for Jack.

Michael Fry

Michael Fry played Jack Manning in the premiere production of Charitable Intent *at La Mama Theatre in Carlton, Melbourne.*

What most struck you about the play on first reading?

My first impression was that Bryony is an out-and-out bully, Amanda is telling the truth and was systematically victimised by Bryony and the gang of three (eventually four, to lesser or greater extents), and Brian was probably more likely to be aware of Bryony's tactics and behaviour than not, but chose to, if not encourage it, then at best turn a blind eye. Indeed I was quite surprised at our first reading when one of the cast said that he thought Bryony's downfall or revelation was a surprise. I must say that my experience of playing it before an audience was that generally the audience were onto Bryony pretty quickly.

My first response was this play is pretty black and white and the characters were, to my taste, too exaggerated. Did Bryony have to be so completely callous to all and sundry for Williamson to make his point? I felt not. I would have been more interested in exploring people who bully and yet can also display generosity and compassion. That was more my experience from the workplace than the character (Bryony) I read in the script. But again, they're my preferences and I'm not a highly successful playwright. I did trust Williamson and I certainly trusted Tom and he allayed any fears I had early in the process.

As I also said, the script really only informs you of the motives, thoughts, actions, behaviour... of those speaking. In performance and rehearsal, of equal interest was what was happening to those who weren't speaking or how people or groups would react when something was said. This was one of the most commented upon aspects the audience responded to: watching the ripple effect.

The other thing that struck me, when I read the script for the first time, notwithstanding my comments on its obviousness, was the potential for a variety of audience responses. Williamson, to my mind, loves comedy/satire. Clearly though, some people may not find, particularly what happens to Amanda, funny. That excited me, I love plays that allow that variety of response, it makes people respond for themselves and from their own experiences and that's how it should be—particularly a play dealing with the themes of *Charitable Intent*.

How did you research your role for the play?
I read a fantastic book called *Transforming Conflict*! My experience as a convenor has mainly been in the area of business facilitation, i.e. audit facilitation, risk management facilitation, business processes facilitation. Yet I'd had experiences where people were reluctant to contribute through fear of repercussions, and so on. I was aware of the need for a convenor to remain objective and manage the process rather than lead the group to predetermined outcomes and how to manage difficult group dynamics. I was also, I believe, familiar with how voice and body language should be used by the convenor.

The other important research we did in rehearsal was exploring the back stories. We did this by conducting the interviews Jack would have had with the individuals concerned. This was extremely beneficial in informing my starting point, if you like: what *did* Jack know when the curtain went up?

Tell us about your experience of preparing for your role each day— and your observations of how the other actors prepared.
I'm not the type of actor who needs to enter my inner self prior to a performance, and I say that without mocking those who do. Each to their own. My preparation was generally chatting with the other cast members—many of us knew each other well and had worked together previously, and we all got on famously. So we'd chat and joke, have a few cigarettes and a cup of tea. I guess this relaxes me and it helps me focus in on where people are: less the character and more the actor, if that makes sense.

I'd see what sort of mood people were in and how the group of us were reacting to each other. If we were in a playful, silly, jokey mood (often), then I'd somehow let that inform me—again less as Jack and more as Michael, the actor. I'd try to use what we had for the performance. I'll give you an example: Vivienne, who played Bryony, has the most delicious and wicked sense of humour. If Viv was in that playful, almost reckless, type of mood, I'd use that. I'd bring it onto the stage. It may be just a glance or an inflection that might register between us and as characters it would add a frisson to our relationship, Jack and Bryony. I'd like to have Viv thinking 'What's Jack playing at?'

It worked for the characters. I think Bryony uses charm and seduction generally as a weapon in all her communication, it seemed an interesting idea to play with that, to be her foil or her ally, to keep her guessing, both as Jack and between us as actors. It worked in with the text and hopefully it added to the texture of the performances.

I would also do a voice warm-up, which involved about 10-minutes of vocal exercises to cover projection, resonance and enunciation. Then, as a group, we would all assemble at 'the beginners'. (This is the call from stage management to the cast for those who are beginning the play to standby. It is usually given 5-minutes before curtain-up.) We would then do a group clap. A clap would be passed around the circle, you have to make eye-contact to pass and receive the clap. You can direct it to anyone. It's a great warm-up to really switch on mentally and to feel a sense of teamwork. It's very energising. We began it early in the season and I think there may have been a night or two when we didn't do our 'clap' and generally the feeling was the show wasn't up to the standard we wanted, so it pretty quickly became an essential part of our preparation.

As Jack, I would enter with the audience and set up the Conference area, make myself a cup of tea, sit down, prepare my notes, etc. I loved this part. It allowed me to switch into that calm and sense of anticipation. I guess convenors, trainers, presenters and actors experience that moment just before 'you're on' and you are the focus and the driver of a process. It was very familiar to me in my experience as an actor and a corporate trainer.

I guess for the others particularly they had to focus on what we call 'the stakes'. These people have a lot at stake prior to the Conference. Tom reminded us that, despite a veneer of confidence or imperturbability, everybody had a story they wanted heard or not revealed, that alliances could shift, in effect everybody was acutely tuned in to what might eventuate. This quality drove the momentum of the play and the performance. As soon as anything was uttered, there was a vital need to respond, react, deflect, pacify, rebut, whatever.

What, for you, were the most memorable audience responses to the play?

Generally, people would say things like, 'I had a boss just like her' or 'I know someone like that' or 'That happened to me', and then proceed to tell you their story. I guess, particularly at La Mama, there was a confessional atmosphere and, I guess, I was seen as the Father Confessor. I don't know, maybe I managed to convince people in the audience that I cared. Funny that.

As to most memorable, I think Tom had a gentleman say to him that they sacked the wrong person. Bryony was fine, it's the Amandas of the world that cause all the trouble with their whinging and 'playing victim' mentality. Business requires ruthlessness sometimes and besides Williamson is a dyed-in-the-wool pinko. (Not his words exactly, I paraphrase.)

To go back to my initial comments about my preferring Bryony to be less overtly demonic, that was not the audiences' experience, it seemed to me. (That's why David lives at Noosa and I live in Northcote.) I still do wish that we had explored a truer face of bullying.

Your situation playing the convenor here is a little unusual insofar as you facilitate in workplaces outside the theatre. Any comments?

Well, I've never had to facilitate a workplace conflict as such. Just enough to persuade Tom that I was perfect for the part!

Andrew Doyle

Andrew Doyle played Luka in the premiere production of Face to Face *and was Assistant Director in the premiere production of* A Conversation.

How different was the experience of acting in *Face to Face* from that of acting in other plays?

The experience was different on a number of levels. I would say it was the most challenging piece of theatre I have done so far. Sandra Bates wanted to make it as real as possible for the audience, wanted them to believe that they were seeing an actual community Conference. She divided the dressing rooms into two distinct camps and fifteen minutes prior to the show we became our characters and only spoke to those people who our character would speak to. All this was a new and exciting experience for me as an actor, not having the safety of a dressing room or the charm of a set and mood lighting to enhance one's performance. It was raw, real theatre.

Throughout the rehearsal period we did a number of improvisations to understand the process behind setting up a Community Conference. Every actor—in character—had an interview with Jack Manning about what was going to happen and what background information we could bring to help resolve the dispute. We role-played a number of the pivotal situations that are talked about during the play (Glen's night at the dogs, Luka being stirred by his mates, etc.) so that each actor had a history and an understanding of the particular situation. Emotionally, it was probably the most draining play I have done.

The great thing about this play was that it could be performed anywhere. A room, a hall, a theatre... didn't matter, and to any amount of people, and the reaction was universally the same. Because of its lack of 'theatricality' and therefore its realism, audiences went on the journey with you to an amazing degree—more than any other play I've done.

The character of Luka makes a series of statements that broaden the scope of the conversation in *Face to Face*. What do you remember about these moments and what for you, are Luka's, and the play-more-generally's, most memorable lines?

The character of Luka is important for the play, because through him and his confessions the audience begin to understand that everything is not black and white and that, while Glen is the one 'on trial', that is because of a number of events to which he was the unwitting party.

When I was performing the role of Luka I felt there were three defining moments for him.

Firstly the telling of 'the joke'. I felt it was important that Luka told the story without a great deal of malice—it was just boys having a laugh—but with a total lack of understanding of the consequences it would eventually have and the number of people it would affect . The image I always had in mind was that of an out-of-control train. Luka's defence is that 'everyone takes the piss out of everyone all the bloody time. It's the only way to stay sane'.

Of course we soon realise that there is another underlying reason. This is the second pivotal moment. The fact that Luka used to be 'the Glen' of Baldoni's—the butt of everyone's jokes—and the fact that it had a great deal to do with his ethnic background. One of our performances of *Face to Face* was actually held at a construction worksite where there was indeed a Serb scaffolder. The stories he related to me about ethnic bullying were truly dreadful and gave me a wonderful insight into how Luka would've felt. The description by Luka of his life and how he feels about himself gives some insight into why he did what he did. The relief for Luka that someone new had joined Baldoni's and could be the butt of everyone's jokes far outweighed his concern for the consequences.

However, by the end of the play, Luka does realise that, because of this Conference, he has been shown the consequences of his actions and the number of people that have been affected, and this is the third pivotal moment. For Luka to apologise to Glen clears the way for Glen to apologise to Mr Baldoni, and for resolutions to be sought.

I think at the end of the play Glen and Luka have an understanding that they are not too dissimilar and that, if there were a *Face to Face 2*, they would be good friends.

Luka's most memorable lines are any of his hugging lines: 'What is this? The fuckin' girl guides? I'm not apologising. I'm not going to start hugging everyone!' 'Jesus, is there normally so much friggin' hugging and shit?' 'Shit, no hugs mate!!'

Diane Craig

Diane Craig played Barbara Milsom in the premiere production of A Conversation. *She had earlier played the role of Maureen Tregaskis in a regional tour of the premiere production of* Face to Face.

The way we came to *Face to Face* was that I had been in Sydney for a while working, and I'd gone back down to the country when I got a call from the Ensemble Theatre saying the production was about to close and there were a couple of tickets for me. I had vaguely heard that it had done fantastic business and had been a sell-out season. And I thought, 'Isn't that strange? It was doing really good business, why are they ringing around trying to give tickets away?'.

Anyway, Garry [McDonald] was up in Sydney, and I told him that

Ensemble had given me some tickets but I didn't want to go back to Sydney for a night. He said that he would go and see it. He saw the second last night that it was on in Sydney, so unfortunately I didn't get a chance to see it after that, because I haven't heard him rave so much about something he'd seen in the theatre for ages. He was so excited he couldn't sleep for two nights! He said, 'It was just fantastic! Everyone in it was so good, and it was so moving, and it was so funny! It was just the most exciting thing I've seen in the theatre for ages'.

So then, of course, I was kicking myself that I hadn't gone to see it. But what I didn't realise was that the reason Sandra [Bates] had rung up about the ticket was that it had been mooted already that it would tour. Sandra had known that certain members of the cast wouldn't be able to go on the tour, so she was looking around for prospective people to go into it. So when the part did become available I said yes. That was how we first came to the Ensemble.

And it was fantastic to travel around the country with it. The audience reaction everywhere we went was just so good. It was fantastic. So then I heard *Face to Face* was part of a trilogy and the second one came along. That was a while after *Face to Face* had finished, and Sandra sent an early draft of *A Conversation*—to Garry and I both, actually—wanting to know if we were interested in doing the husband and wife together. I must say, when we first read the early draft of it, we thought, 'Oh my God, this is so bleak! It's so *unrelentingly* bleak'. Where *Face to Face* has so much humour in it as well as the other stuff that was going on, we just couldn't imagine it here.

But Williamson's plays are fascinating like that. You read them on the page and it's so difficult to see everything that's there and how audiences are going to react to them. The audience finds so much there that they can identify with and relate to, and it just speaks to people so clearly. It's extraordinary.

But reading *Conversation*, we just couldn't imagine that there could be any laughs in it at all. How could anyone *possibly* laugh in the middle of all this dreadful sadness? But amazingly, once it went in front of audiences, there were laughs in it. I suppose like the Shakespearian tragedies, there's alway that comic relief. You have to give the audience a moment or two to get a break from all that. There were a couple of points that you could say, when you first read the script, 'Oh yeah, well, that's obviously a "joke"—but will anyone laugh at it!?' There were maybe two things in it that were amusing. But no, there was much more than that in the end, much more. Audiences need that release.

What were the differences in audience reactions to the two plays?
With _Conversation_, one or two people would walk out—not a lot of people, sometimes just one person, or you might get a couple of people—because it was just so confronting. Sometimes you just touch too raw a nerve and people just can't stay. They can't take it in.

With _Face to Face_ there was never anything like that. When you do these country tours, of course, you quite often get the chance to meet with the audience afterwards. They provide suppers. They love to do all that, which is fabulous. I can remember, for instance, when we went to Shepparton, there were a lot of people there that night who work at the canning factory and who all came up and said, 'Look, those people are just _so_ typical, and the situation is just _so_ typical of the things that go on'. And you'd get an awful lot of that as you'd go around the country.

With _Conversation_, when we did the opening night, we were so unsure as to what the response would be. A woman came up to me in the foyer on opening night. She looked vaguely familiar, and she came up to me and the first thing she said to me was 'My daughter was murdered…'., and I thought, 'My God, this poor woman's just sat through this play!' And she said to me, '…and I have been through one of these Conferences'.

And then, as she talked to me, it suddenly fell into place. Geoff [Cartwright] had various tapes of people who had been through Conferences—and we had watched her and her husband doing interviews. She said to me, 'You know, you captured what it was like very truthfully'. So I was pretty gratified by that.

There was another night, which was really difficult, because we had the Homicide Victims' Support Group, about thirty or forty people. I don't know why you would put yourself through that. I think they were people who had heard about Conferencing but had not yet decided whether they actually wanted to go through the process or not. And some of those I spoke to in the foyer afterwards decided that it wasn't for them—but probably because they hadn't had the distance of time yet.

The opening night for _Conversation_ was quite astonishing really. We got a standing ovation, which I'd never expected. People thought it was terrific. I didn't really go into it in great detail with people, because, when I'd finished that play, the last thing I wanted was to turn around and talk to people about it. But the response from people when we'd finished was extraordinary, and the buzz in the foyer afterwards was fairly amazing. So it obviously struck a chord with people.

Before the play, I had actually seen that documentary they showed on the ABC, *Facing the Demons*. I just came across it one night on the television, out of the blue, not knowing anything about it, and I just found it riveting to watch, fascinating television and fascinating real life drama. That was another thing that we then went back and had a look at when we were researching *A Conversation*. It's obviously such a fantastic process, and so useful to people, and so helpful, even to people who have gone through such horrific experiences. It can bring them some sort of... peace—which is a word that several of those people I spoke with used. And it's so good as an actor to be involved with something that can be promoting what is obviously such a worthwhile thing for people to be doing. It's not very often as an actor that you get an opportunity to do things like that which you feel are so worthwhile.

What was the hardest part, technically, about performing *A Conversation*?
Probably having to reproduce it every day, as it was so highly emotionally charged; just having to put yourself through that everyday—twice on Thursdays and twice on Saturdays! Some of the cast would perhaps say that they enjoyed it, but I know a lot of them would say they found it *very* difficult. I don't think that I could do it again.

Another of the difficult things about doing *A Conversation* was the research. I did a bit of background reading, getting into a world that is just so far removed from the world that we live in. I read *Somebody Else's Daughter*, the book on Anita Cobby's murder, and it was just so frightening, getting into that world. I found that book so totally shocking. Being a mother myself, having a grown-up daughter, having spent sleepless nights when they were in their late teens going out to night clubs, and lying in bed at two o'clock in the morning hearing sirens going down the road and thinking, 'Please God, let that not be my child being carted off to the hospital or the police station!'—not that my kids ever got into trouble like that but it's the sort of thing that goes through your mind as a parent. And having to get into that world of the sort of people who would do that was just so frightening.

Geoff was a wonderful source of material for all this. I went looking for a book by Anita Cobby's father, because I'd heard that he had written a book and I wanted to get the parent's perspective. The book was actually written with someone else, and once we started rehearsals, I got the book, *Struck By Lightning*, from Geoff. It was an extraordinary book, I thought.

And I suppose, as an actor, you do tend to relate things in the play to your own life, and I guess, playing that part, I would think of my daughter a lot. So it was just really hard dredging all that up every day for however many weeks it was that we did it... So when Sandra started talking about touring it a while ago, at first I thought, 'If it tours, I suppose I should do it'. Then the more I thought about it, the more I thought, 'I really don't think I *could* do it again'. So I might have to just let that go...

How did the experience of watching *Charitable Intent* compare with playing in *Face to Face* and *A Conversation*?
I happened to see *Charitable Intent* with a friend who was going through something similar, in Melbourne, at the time. And she found it terribly relevant. She thoroughly enjoyed it. I don't know that the play is actually quite as good as the first two. But certainly the audience that we saw it with in Melbourne were just as enthusiastic as audiences in Sydney, and this girl I saw it with found it extremely relevant.

Rhonda Booby

Rhonda Booby founded the Restorative Justice Unit within the NSW Department of Corrections

What are your key memories of *A Conversation*?
My memories are vague now, not only given the time that has passed since the play, but also because I have experienced a number of real-life Conferences. So my memories are probably corrupted (or enhanced) by what I have observed at other Conferences. I don't think much can be made of my 'raw' memories. For what they are worth—here's what comes to mind:

- ◆ the pain of the parents of the victim;
- ◆ the strain on the relationship of the parents of the victim;
- ◆ the difficulty experienced by the father of the victim in accessing his feelings;
- ◆ the sense of purpose of the offender's family—whilst they still had their anguish and conflicts they could work together as a unit to

help the offender. This is something we often find—the victim families are left with a 'gap' to fill, an emptiness, whereas the offender's family has a focus for action. Look at the recent publicity given to the mother of the rapist because she has had difficulty in visiting her son; and

♦ the relief experienced by everyone after they had said what they had to say.

How realistic did you find the Conference?

The Conference was quite realistic except that on the first night the script involved the facilitator being aware of the fact that the motivation for the family of the offender was that they wanted the victim's family to sign their petition. As I said to David Williamson, we would not have Conferenced if this was their motivation. Williamson later changed the script so that the facilitator did not know about this motivation (I think they did not even know about the petition), but I would be disappointed if in one of our Conferences a petition existed but one of our facilitators had not picked up on the existence of the petition nor thoroughly analysed the offender's family's motivation.

If a petition existed we certainly would have discussed this with the victim's family in the context of whether they wanted to go ahead with the Conference knowing that the offender's family's motivation might be related to the petition, or might be about improving things generally for the offender. For example, if an offender seeks to Conference whilst an appeal or classification process is pending we would advise the victim of this fact and give them the opportunity of Conferencing now or after the finalisation of the process. This avoids the victim feeling 'used' afterwards.

I found the prison psychologist quite unrealistic. I can barely contemplate a situation in which a prison psychologist would assess an inmate as appropriate for release where s/he really thought there was a high likelihood of a re-offence of this nature (except perhaps in the case of some romantic relationship developing—these are rare, but do happen, although more often in fiction than real life).

Also, as you would be aware, we have never conducted a Conference in the absence of the offender. It is interesting to ponder whether we would. Whilst it would be somewhat outside our brief—given that offenders are our 'stock in trade'—I can contemplate a situation where the offender's and victim's families might ask us to facilitate a Conference, say where they lived in close proximity and the offender was incarcerated for a lengthy period. However an issue would be about how such a Conference would affect the relationship and understanding between the family's of the victim and of the offender, leaving the offender out of the loop, and probably even more estranged from his family and therefore even less able to adapt to family life upon his release.

Can a play like this assist the mission of the Unit?

Undoubtedly, though its reach is quite small. It would be fantastic for us if it were made into a movie! However, as you know, people take a lot of convincing about the value of open communication in this format and even the middle class audience of a David Williamson play would not immediately see the value of a Conference under such emotional circumstances. We need to reach as many people as possible with this play and the messages that come out of it.

There are two sides that need convincing—those who see victims as needing support and assistance and who view Conferences as potentially traumatic for the victims, and those who are pro-offender rights and see Conferences as inappropriately involving victims in the criminal justice system which should be left to courts, lawyers and offenders. Then of course there are those (many) who shy away from expressions of emotions and believe that things are better left unexplored and unsaid. Any measures that address the thinking of these people help to promote Conferencing, and the play did this very well.

Members of the Homicide Victims' Support Group

Martha Jabour is the Executive Director of the Homicide Victims' Support Group (Aust) Inc., a position she has held for the past ten years. She arranged this conversation with colleagues and group members in May 2002. Sharondell Baggott works for the HVSG in an administrative role doing special projects. Maria Fraser's three children were murdered. Michael Fazio's mother was murdered by his father in a murder suicide. Alex Faraguna is a grief counsellor with the HVSG. Trudy Adelstein is a grief counsellor with the HVSG. Jacqui Stanton works with the HVSG as an administrative assistant and database co-ordinator. Noreen Berrett's son was murdered by a juvenile.

Martha: Six months after you all saw *A Conversation*, what do you remember most about the experience?

Sharondell: The one thing that still sticks in my craw today is the way that the mother admitted to those people that her daughter wasn't perfect. 'She did this and that'—whatever it was. Remember how she describes the way her daughter had painted the kitchen yellow? Now I don't know if that was the way it was written, or just what I picked up…

Maria: But I thought that showed the similarities between the two families. They come together, they haven't necessarily resolved anything, but they are both shattered by what the perpetrator did. And they are blaming the other parties, blaming each other. I think that's normal. You ask yourself why you didn't do this or that… Even the brother says 'People see me as a rapist!' Even though he wasn't the one committing these crimes, he's still blamed… And that's actually the mentality in our [South East Asian] culture: if someone does the wrong thing, others say, 'You have to keep away from this family!'

Martha: That's true, but I think it's also true in every culture.

Michael: It is, and that's the sad thing about it. People are simplistic… I think they tend to associate people's behaviour with their upbringing, and so associate them with the family.

Maria: There wasn't much mention of the father in *A Conversation*. The main male figure of the play was the uncle.

Sharondell: Wouldn't you assume that Scott was, in effect, the man of the house, at the time? The uncle certainly takes care of the money side, but the offender was the man around the house. He was certainly the apple of his mother's eye… she was feeling guilty for not providing the perfect family, or not having the time because she was trying to…

Martha: Which is the sad bit we don't see… I mean, you'll find very often that the offender's side will support the offender, they'll come to court every day, they'll be just so supportive, and very often the victim's side will think, 'How could they support him?'. But you don't know the reasons behind why they are supportive…

Alex: …until you read that book! Jefferey Dahmers' father, Lionel Dahmer, wrote a book, *A Father's Story*. You can't put it down. It really helps you to understand why offenders' families support them the way they do. They've had a whole lifelong relationship with them. That was their baby; that was their toddler. Lionel Dahmer says, 'Well, he wet the bed when he was six. Should I have known then that there was something wrong? Was there something I did or something I didn't do?' It was almost like a confession.

Maria: And that's how it was with Coral in this play. She really feels guilty that she wasn't around to instil discipline.

Martha: And she was doing her best to give them a decent upbringing so that they wouldn't have to do bad things to survive… Quite recently one of the family members of our group went to a Conference. It was a really positive Conference, and the convenor felt that that person's got a lot out of it, and there was an outcome plan, because the person's coming out on parole soon. And I met the offender, and we talked about it, me being on the panel, and I asked him how had he found it. He said, 'It's probably one of the worst things I've ever done in my life. I've felt so bad'. And I asked, 'What's made you feel so bad?' He replied, 'Just seeing the pain of the family'. And I thought, 'That's a positive thing in itself, because I'm just hoping he comes out and never, ever touches a fly'. So that's a positive outcome, because, yes he'd had a bad childhood; he'd had a terrible childhood, and gone off and murdered one of his friends. So you don't see the other side.

Michael: But that's that same old environmental excuse.

Alex: And what about all those who've had a bad childhood who don't murder?

Martha: That's true, and that's how you have to put it into perspective: 'No matter how your childhood was, it gives you no excuse to murder'. And he's actually felt worse, for the pain that he's caused. And the family have accepted that. The family of the victim actually felt a whole lot better hearing that from him, as opposed to being left wondering, 'Well, how does he feel about killing our son?'.

Alex: They probably assumed he didn't give a toss about it.

Sharondell: Martha, what's the percentage of murders that are truly calculated, as against 'a crime of passion?'.

Martha: Eighty percent are committed by someone known to the victim. Sixty percent are domestic murders.

Michael: I'm in a bit of a unique situation there. I can't attend a Conference [as my parents are part of that statistic].

Sharondell: What I'm saying is you could *possibly* forgive somebody who was drunk and fighting with their wife, or who was on drugs and fighting with their girlfriend, but something that was a calculated murder you wouldn't be able to forgive.

Trudy: I don't see why you should forgive anyone who murders, even in a blind rage. Because why do they need to get that enraged?

Sharondell: Well, obviously Derek didn't seem to be understanding how it could have happened, but the mother, Barbara, seemed to be understanding it… whereas Derek didn't move. At the end of the play he was concerned not to be going soft on… You wouldn't care, would you?

Noreen: No.

Alex: And I think a lot of people would feel the same way as Noreen.

Martha: But in a factual sense, that wouldn't be an issue that you'd be considering in the Conference. Michael, how did you feel about the play, knowing that you could never attend a Conference?

Michael: That's one of the things I found most interesting, it portrayed something that has helped me deal with it, which is that, if you understand a bit about what happened, and if you understand what's going through that person's mind, at least you can say, alright, I see what was going on. So you do reach a point where, though you can never forget, you sort of forgive in the sense of saying, at least I know what caused it. But if you're going to keep thinking about what's happened, having to ask yourself why, and blame someone, there's no point, because it's not just one person. And that's what's portrayed so well in the play: a lot of things have led to this.

Sharondell: How did that play make you realise why the person did it?

Michael: Well, the play didn't, because at a very young age I'd already learned to gather as much factual information as I could about how my mother and my father died—because they both died on the same day. I understood a lot about what had happened, but our situation was unusual as well because my sister and I already somehow predicted what was going to happen, and prepared ourselves psychologically for it… She's still very angry in a way, whereas somehow I've accepted it.

Martha: But these domestic murders are different. And they're the ones in particular where you do ask yourself as a family member, 'What could I have done to have prevented it?'. If it's random, there are a lot of ifs, whats and whys. But because they're random, you can't focus on, 'Well, I should have seen it coming'.

Alex: But what I hear from mothers a lot is 'Why didn't I teach my daughter to look after herself?'. When there's no logical objective reason for guilt, that's the one that will come up…

Sharondell: But why in this play was the mother virtually saying, 'I can understand why she was killed? Because she was pigheaded, and stubborn, and she wasn't perfect'. She wasn't asking 'why?'

Jacqui: I don't recall her doing that. I remember her being more compassionate, more forgiving. But I don't remember her putting her daughter down. I don't remember that.

Martha: I thought the mother had processed things a lot more. The father hadn't really looked at why he was angry.

Michael: He hadn't let go.

Martha: It was too painful for him to go there. Because a couple of times he got up and he'd say, 'That's it, I've had enough; I'm going!'.

Maria: I don't think he had actually gone through the phase of grieving.

Alex: And in a way he didn't want to hear.

Sharondell: But why didn't she talk about when she took her first steps, or when she got an A in her maths? Why didn't she talk about her achievements?

Jacqui: I remember very clearly the relationship between the parents. They were very conflicting. In my experience, a lot of families want to remember, they want to talk about their child, and their life, all those happy nice things, and that's what keeps them going… But Derek had problems with that side of it. He didn't want to, he was very reserved: 'I don't need to talk about this; they don't need to know.'

Alex: I think Sharondell's right though, particularly if they were talking about the victim to the offender's family, they would be talking in glowing terms about her. I don't think they would say anything negative in front of the offender's family, even if with a counsellor they could talk about the good and the bad.

Maria: But it's true that people handle their grief quite differently. She does seem ready to move on, but maybe because he hasn't grieved…

Sharondell: Derek's character is very easy to understand, because he's still right there, where it happened, and he may never move.

Michael: I think the way he put it was very good. She wasn't an angel. But she didn't deserve to be murdered. No one deserves to be murdered.

Sharondell: I must have missed her verbalising that. [See page 67 of *A Conversation*.] I think she was doing it to make Coral feel better.

Alex: But what else did she say about her daughter that was a bit negative—apart from her behaviour at the birthday party?

Various: They were only little comments.

Jacqui: I didn't even take those comments as being negative…

Trudy: I think she's actually saying that my daughter was just normal like everybody else.

Maria: Yes, that she was strong-willed, but that's normal.

Jacqui: And then you had to feel sorry for the younger brother... for the way his life was affected by it.

Martha: For every line in that play, I could honestly say that I've heard it from a family.

Various: Yes, that's true. That's how it was.

Martha: The impact of it was so overwhelming, it took me weeks to recover, because I'd just keep hearing the families that I'd been with, who'd said those different lines. I'd seen the families put down their kids, and I'd seen the families that could never remember a single thing that their children did that was wrong. And then you see the offender's side—and I have spoken to some offenders' families—and I think 'You poor buggers; I don't know how you're going to survive'. I hadn't spoken about this with offenders until quite recently, and that's a different experience altogether. But we did talk here in the office for weeks and weeks and weeks about just how real it was.

Sharonodelle: Well, I spent most of the night trying to calm down the lady next to me. She was crying the whole way through it, the poor thing. It took me a good hour and a half afterwards to calm her down....

Martha: Her son was murdered by his flatmate, a person they knew very well.

Michael: You think about how much trust had gone out the window, because they'd probably trusted this guy with everything, and then they think, 'Well, who else can we trust?' That should be understood—how everything is interdependent. In my case it's a little different, the problem's more that a lot of people stereotype you. People say, your father was like that, so you must be, and that's the sad thing about it. People whose relative is killed in a random shooting are asking something a little bit different. They're simply asking '*Why* did that happen?'.

Martha: Sharondell, the character you remember most was the victim's mother, and Jaqui, you most remember the offender's brother...

Jaqui: ... because I saw a lot of pain.

Martha: What about the others?

Alex: The offender's sister, and partly because she brought the light relief. So many of the things she said were, frankly, dumb, and so, funny. But also because we hear that kind of thing a lot—the bad childhood, this and that other excuses, and... 'Shutup!' You do hear that.

Maria: I remember *everyone*: for the dialogue, and the conversation that emerged between them… and the emotions which the characters shared.

Michael: And I must say, that made me feel relieved, in a way. I suppose I shouldn't use the word, but I found the play 'enjoyable', in the sense that it portrayed so much so well that you thought and felt, 'Well, at least someone else understands!' And that's the way I really felt. 'There is hope!'

Martha: For me it was the psychologist. I felt so sorry for her. I felt, 'God! To actually be in that position where you've written that report, and the guilt that you must feel now'. It could be anyone of us.

Sharondell: But I didn't see that she'd done her job well, because she let this perpetrator just charm her in, so instead of being objective…

Alex: Perhaps the play should be performed for psychologists and psychiatrists as a warning! I felt sorry for her, and I thought, after seeing that, 'How could you do a job like that? How could you be responsible for letting a murderer out, knowing he might kill again?'

Maria: But she believed that anyone could change. She believed in the human spirit… coming into play.

Martha: The reality is, in our criminal justice system, ninety eight percent of offenders will come out of jail.

Alex: And that makes sense, doesn't it, because when you're on parole you get intense supervision, and if you're not on parole, you don't. So you might as well…

Sharondell: I see it a little different to that. From where I worked in the past, as you know, the boys had committed heinous crimes. And if you were to ask me, logically, I would say not one of these kids had a chance from the day they were born. And my heart went out to all of them. However, when I left, I recommended non-release for any of them. They were never taught any guilt, never had any conscience. It was too late. By the time we got them it was too late to retrain them. Maybe one, possibly, out of seventy-five, I could possibly see. One of chaps actually broke out of the centre—he was in there for raping an elderly lady in a nursing home—he got out of the centre, robbed someone at the station to get money to get on the train, and attacked them with an axe. And he still couldn't see what he had done was wrong when he was recaptured. It was his right to get out of there, get the money… So I think a lot of it's got to do with this having no conscience.

Martha: That's the beauty of the *youth justice* conferencing. The fact that you're bringing these young people face to face with their victim when they've just committed a serious enough crime...

Sharondell: Well, they realise the victim's a person...

Martha: ... so you're diverting young people from that cycle.

Sharondell: Okay, so why was Scott the bad guy in that play? Was it because he had no conscience? Was it his upbringing?

Martha: Maybe, his mother couldn't see him doing anything wrong.

Maria: She often wasn't there. And then his brother says, even when she is, 'You don't see how bad he is!'...

Martha: A question to all of you, as people who know more about this subject than other members of the audience could: what do you see as the use of a play like *A Conversation*?

All: Education! Public education!

Noreen: Yes, education, though I wouldn't want to attend a Conference in my case. Not even with the family. Because there have been four murders from two sons in this family...

Sharondell: So who stuck in your mind?

Noreen: I was watching the victim couple, how they reacted to each other, how it was *so* true. It's just like my husband and I and that 'Don't talk about it!' You tend to talk to somebody else about it.

Sharondell: So from the play you assumed that Barbara and Derek hadn't communicated about it...

Noreen: Yes, and that's how it is...

Martha: And there's no reason for Noreen to want to sit across from this guy and ask 'Why?'—which is what a lot of our families do want to ask. 'Why didn't you kill yourself?'

Maria: ... And there probably will never be an answer. You can keep on waiting and asking, 'Why not me?', 'Why am I alone?', 'What motivates you?' There are so many answers. We might speculate. And even if they tell us, we still don't know whether that is the right reason.

Michael: I suppose that's where I was lucky, living with my father, I knew what was going through his head.

Maria: For me, I thought I could read it... I thought I knew the person very well.

Michael: And with my father, also, he was pretty verbal, and you could also read a lot into his body language. I realised later he'd had psychotic episodes. Though it's no use making excuses.

Sharondell: But I don't think the guy in the play was psychotic; he was just a bully.

Martha: He was a murderer, and a double rapist! And there is a long, technical argument about different modes of treatment. How well do people remember the contrast and debate between aggressive 'deconditioning therapy' and Lorin's gentler 'talking therapy'?

Various: Not well.

Maria: What I remember is the way in which he was able to manipulate the psychologist...

Martha: Derek did have all his paperwork...

Sharondell: But he was hard to listen to. He was so angry, and yelling, that you just shut right down. He was so angry. And see, had it been a general discussion, you probably would have been interested in listening. But everyone, when someone yells at you, you stop listening... Still, people are like that. I think I would be.

Trudy: And this debate is something he's got control over, that's a way of looking at it. He wants to have some type of control, because he hasn't had any other type of control in his life. And he's able to say, 'I've done this research, look how well I've done! ... And nobody's listening to me'.

Michael: It was meant to be intimidating—and that's his strength, to be intimidating, instead of being understanding.

Martha: And a lot of people do that...

Michael: ... because you're weak in so many other ways.

Sharondell: Then, you see, Jacqui felt sorry for the brother. My sense was that the brother felt relieved that he got [Scott] out of his hair and could live a normal life now without being bullied by Scott... Well, we all see things differently... I met a lady about a month ago at a function, and she mentioned that she'd been to see *A Conversation*. And I got a shock, because she *chose* to go and see it. And it made a huge impact on her—that this actually does happen. It's not just in the movies. It actually happens to people in real life.

5. Questions for discussion

The following questions are useful prompts for individual analysis or group discussion of the plays in *The Jack Manning Trilogy*.

In *Face to Face*, two scaffolders, Nookie Finlay and Mac, have been involved in the conflict at Baldoni's, but they don't attend the Conference. Glen's sister also doesn't attend because 'she's still so mad' at him.

◆ How might the Conference have unfolded differently had Nookie and Mac attended? How might the Conference have unfolded differently had Glen's sister attended?

◆ Who else might have attended the Conference in *A Conversation* and *Charitable Intent*, and how might their attendance have influenced the process and the outcome?

◆ What ideas do participants use to attack other participants, and what defences do those who are under attack employ?

Director Tom Gutteridge describes an exercise with the cast of *Charitable Intent* in which 'peacemakers ...[get] between antagonists who might be physically wrestling'.

◆ For each play, plot the sequence in which conflict moves around the circle, as participants become overtly antagonistic to one another.

◆ Identify specific examples of peacemaking.

◆ Which conflicts between groups exacerbate the conflict between *individuals* in each of these plays?

◆ What key lines prompt emotional steps forward?

David Williamson cites the term 'collective vulnerability' when describing the turning point in a Conference.

◆ Identify the moment(s) of 'collective vulnerability' in each play.

◆ What prompts these moments?

◆ Where do they lead?

Consider the following excerpt from *A Conversation* [p.67]:

BARBARA: When Donna was in primary school the teacher said, 'Yeah she's bright, but look at this'. And she showed us a sociogram. A graph with arrows showing which kids wanted to be friends with which. And all the arrows—
DEREK: Pointed to Donna.

Jacob Moreno, the Austrian-born founder of 'psychodrama', developed the sociogram or sociograph to analyse the role of individuals in groups. Peter O'Connell, of the Hunter Valley Research Foundation, prepared a series of sociographs to analyse the changes that occur in Baldoni's in the lead up to the *Face to Face* Conference.[39] This exercise in 'diagnostic sociometry' is equally fruitful for *A Conversation* and *Charitable Intent*.

Moreno's technique is informed by that invaluable principle of making things as simple as possible, but no simpler. Thus, he designates an interpersonal relationship at any given time as positive, neutral, or negative. In the terminology I have suggested above, a positive relationship prompts *constructive engagement*, a neutral relationship involves *passive disengagement*, and a negative relationship prompts *active disengagement* and/or *destructive engagement*.

In the following sociographs, the three types of relationship are represented with these symbols:

Of course, many relationships are asymmetrical. One party may be attracted to the other, but the other may be indifferent ('neutral'), and so on. The symbols represent these relationships in the following way:

The two sociographs that appear on page 84 are prepared by Peter O'Connell, and represent, in sequence:

◆ the established culture at Baldoni's,
◆ the situation after Glen realises what has been happening and lashes out at Richard and Greg.

The established culture at Baldoni's

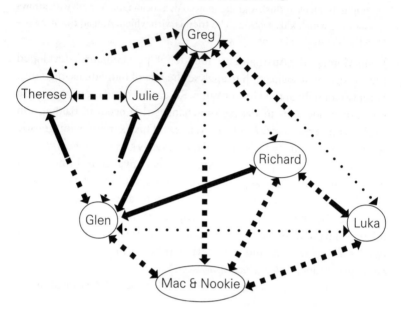

The situation after Glen has lashed out at Richard and Greg

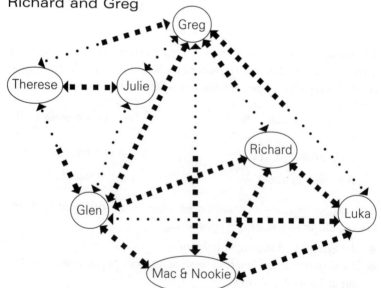

This visual representation of a changing situation makes it quite clear why Richard and Greg are the prime targets of Glen's rage. These were the two people with whom Glen thought he had positive relationships, even while others were making his life difficult. As Glen realises that he's been a laughing stock for the whole workplace, he likewise becomes aware that he there isn't a single positive relationship binding him to the place. He is alone.

What is *not* shown here is a sociograph mapping the relationships that are possible if participants successfully implement the Agreement they reach in *Face to Face*.

Prepare a sociograph for each play of the trilogy, mapping relationships at three stages of the Conference: before, during, and after.

6. The critics

The following quotations convey, in sequence, a sense of the critical reception to *The Jack Manning Trilogy*:

◆ 'A raw, compassionate and timely play.'
   Bryce Hallett, *Sydney Morning Herald*, 22 March 1999

◆ 'You can laugh from a great height at its theatricality, or you can let yourself be drawn into its emotional narrative.'
   John McCallum, 'Somewhere between Satire and Sympathy', *Australian*, 22 March 1999

◆ 'It is nothing short of a miracle to see how such a subtle pattern, wherein every character gets his legitimate opportunity to reveal himself in a protected environment, has been created.... Nine nervous people enter and, after 90 minutes, emerge changed forever.'
   Carol Payne, *North Shore Times*, 24 March 1999

◆ 'Sandra Bate's clear and intelligent production again eschews theatrical artifice in favour of austerity and narrowing the actor-audience relationship.'
   Bryce Hallett, *Sydney Morning Herald*, 17 September 2001

◆ 'At the end there is a resolution, a new understanding and the beginning of a rather faltering sense of renewal.'
   John McCallum, *Australian*, 24 September 2001

◆ 'In a long career, Williamson has been prone to sudden outbursts of passionate conviction... The conflict is resolved very simply, by a revelation of incompetent management and the moral vindication of the old ways.'
   John McCallum, *Australian*, 12 October 2001

◆ '[Bryony's] "corporate speak" is so breath-taking, so lamentably familiar, so utterly self-serving and narcissistic, that it elicits snorts and guffaws of laughter at every turn. Here we see Williamson's talent for satire at its most devastating.'
   Helen Thomson, *Age*, 12 October 2001

Endnotes

1   Conferencing is now being adopted internationally but the term can describe different, if related, processes. References to Conferencing throughout this text are specifically to the version of Conferencing developed and promulgated by TJA.

2   We began using the phrase 'TJA Conferencing' in 2000 to differentiate the Conferencing format and the training program developed by TJA from other formats and trainings. We had previously used the terms 'community conferencing' and 'workplace conferencing' to distinguish two different applications of the Conferencing process. One application of Conferencing was in educational institutions, justice systems and neighbourhood conflict management programs, where the process was generally provided free of charge. The other main application of Conferencing was in workplaces, where the process was convened as a commercial conflict management service. However, by 2000 the terms 'conferencing', 'community conferencing' and 'workplace conferencing' were being used indiscriminately, for interventions of vastly varying quality. This endangered the reputation of both the Conferencing process and the reputation of those programs that were using Conferencing appropriately. Accordingly, some phrase was required to indicate that a Facilitator had been adequately trained and would convene a very specific type of process, one that had already been thoroughly tested, but was nevertheless subject to ongoing, sophisticated evaluation. Hence the phrase 'TJA Conferencing'.

3   Introduction, David B. Moore & John M. McDonald, *Transforming Conflict*, Sydney: Transformative Justice Australia, 2000.

4   Cited in Brian Kiernan, *David Williamson: A Writer's Career*, Sydney: Currency Press, 1996, p. 111. See also pp. 215–216.

5   This page reference, and all subsequent references to the plays, is from David Williamson, *The Jack Manning Trilogy*, Sydney: Currency Press, 2002.

6   In 1999, when *Face to Face* was written, the only form of Conferencing provided by a government agency in New South Wales, where the play is set, was 'Youth Justice Conferencing', provided for under legislation passed in 1997 and administered from a Directorate within the NSW Department

of Juvenile Justice. However, since Glen is older than eighteen, he would not have been eligible to have his offence dealt with in a Youth Justice Conference. The alternative scenario here is that the Conference is being convened independently of the formal justice system. Since Glen has not committed a 'serious indictable offence', the formal justice system may have no further interest in the matter if all parties affected are able to reach a mutually satisfactory agreement to repair the harm that has been done.

[7]   For further information, see J. Hudson, A. Morris, G. Maxwell, & B. Galaway (eds), *Family Group Conferences: Perspectives on policy and practice*, Sydney: Federation Press, 1996.

[8]   David B. Moore, & John M. McDonald, 'Achieving the Good Community: A local police initiative and its wider ramifications' in Kayleen M. Hazlehurst (ed), *Justice and Reform, Volume 2: Regenerating Communities through Crime Prevention*, Aldershot: Avebury, 1995.

[9]   The original Australian evaluation of Conferencing is available online through the Australian Institute of Criminology. David B. Moore with Lubica Forsythe, *A New Approach to Juvenile Justice: An evaluation of family conferencing in Wagga Wagga*, Wagga: Centre for Rural Social Research, 1995, is available at: www.aic.gov.au/oldreports

[10] Ashkanasy, N., Hartel, C.E.J. and Zerbe, W.J., *Emotions in the Workplace: Research, Theory and Practice*, Westport, CT: Quorum Books, 2000; Lewis, T., Amini, F. and Lannon R., *A General Theory of Love*, New York: Random House, 2000.

[11] David B. Moore, 'Shame, Forgiveness, and Juvenile Justice', *Criminal Justice Ethics*, 12, 1993. Reprinted in M. C. Braswell, B. R. McCarthy & B. J. McCarthy (eds), *Justice, Crime and Ethics*, (2nd ed.), Cincinatti, OH: Anderson Publishing, 1996. Available at www.lib.jjay.cuny.edu/cje/html/sample2.html. See also Moore & McDonald, 'Emotions' in *Transforming Conflict*; and Moore & McDonald, 'Community Conferencing as a Special Case of Conflict Transformation' in John Braithwaite & Heather Strang (eds), *Restorative Justice and Civil Society*, Cambridge: Cambridge University Press, 2001.

[12] See Lily Trimboli, *An Evaluation of the NSW Youth Justice Conferencing Scheme*, NSW Bureau of Crime Statistics and Research, Sydney, 2000; and Garth Luke & Bronwyn Lind, *Reducing Juvenile Crime: Conferencing versus Court*, NSW Bureau of Crime Statistics and Research, Sydney, 2002, both available through www.lawlink.nsw.gov.au, specifically at www.agd.nsw.gov.au/bocsar1.nsf/pages/cjb69text.

[13] Roger Fisher, William Ury & Bruce Patton, *Getting to Yes: Negotiating Without Giving In* (2nd ed.), London: Arrow Books, 1991.

[14] Moore & McDonald, *Transforming Conflict*, pp. 15–23.

[15] G. Burford & J. Hudson (eds), *Family Group Conferences: New Directions in Community-Centered Child and Family Practice*, Hawthorne, NY: Aldine de Gruyter, 2000.

16 John Braithwaite & Heather Strang (eds), *Restorative Justice and Civil Society*, Cambridge: Cambridge University Press, 2001.

17 Moore & McDonald, *Transforming Conflict*, pp. 37–42.

18 David B. Moore, 'The Theatre of Everyday Conflict' in David Williamson, *The Jack Manning Trilogy*, pp. xvi–xx.

19 Kiernan, *David Williamson: A Writer's Career*, p. 227.

20 Bryce Hallett, 'Williamson sparks power play before ink is dry, *Sydney Morning Herald*, 5 September 2002, p. 3.

21 Paul E. Griffiths, *What Emotions Really Are: The Problem of Psychological Categories*. Chicago, University of Chicago Press, 1997. See also the Kings College London Emotions project: www.kcl.ac.uk/ip/nevensesardic

22 M. Gladwell, 'The Naked Face: Can you read people's faces just by looking at them?', *New Yorker*, 5 August 2002, pp. 38–49.

23 New York: Norton, 1992.

24 Silvan S. Tomkins, *Affect, Imagery, Consciousness*, New York: Springer Verlag, 4 vols. 1961–1991. See also V. Demos (ed.), *Exploring Affect: The selected writings of Silvan S. Tomkins*, Cambridge: Cambridge University Press, 1994.

25 David Williamson, 'Introduction', *After the Ball*, Sydney: Currency Press, 1997, p. ix.

26 Moore with Forsythe, *A New Approach to Juvenile Justice*.

27 David B. Moore, 'Affect and Script and the Business World', plenary address to the Tomkins Institute, Colloquium 'Doing Brief Psychotherapy', Philadelphia Museum of Art, October 1996.

28 David Williamson, e-mail correspondence with David Moore 25 November 2000

29 *ibid.*

30 See Moore with Forsythe, *A New Approach to Juvenile Justice*.

31 Kiernan, *David Williamson: A Writer's Career*, p. 279.

32 Kiernan, p. 67.

33 See, for example, the website of University of Minnesota Center for Restorative Justice and Peacemaking, ssw.che.umn.edu/rjp/

34 See Jane Jacobs, *Systems of Survival: A dialogue on the moral foundations of commerce and politics*, London: Hodder and Stoughton, 1992.

35 David Williamson, e-mail correspondence with David Moore 27 August 2001

36 David Williamson, e-mail correspondence with David Moore 28 August 2001

37 Douglas Stone, Bruce Patton & Sheila Heen, *Difficult Conversations: How to discuss what matters most*, New York: Penguin, 1999.

38 For the record, if recollections are accurate, the music was by Norwegian jazz guitarist and composer Terje Rypdal.

39 Peter O'Connell, 2001, 'Sociometry, multi-party dispute and haiku poetry', Paper prepared for Dispute Resolution Course, University of Western Sydney. The following sociographs were all prepared by Peter O'Connell, and are reproduced with his kind permission.

David B. Moore was a founding director of TJA (Transformative Justice Australia), the work of which inspired *The Jack Manning Trilogy*.

David taught politics, history and justice studies at the University of Melbourne and Charles Sturt University, and then worked in the Queensland Premier's Department before co-founding TJA in 1995. He has since worked internationally to bring Conferencing and related processes to workplaces, the justice system, and schools. David has worked with schools and universities in Australia and North America to design conflict management programs, and also with professional actors to dramatise different approaches to conflict in organisations. Since 2002, David has worked as an independent consultant based in Sydney, where he lives with his family.